AMONG THE NOOTKA

The True Adventure of John R. Jewett

GERALD STANLEY

AMONG THE NOOTKA
THE TRUE ADVENTURE OF JOHN R. JEWETT

iUniverse books may be ordered through booksellers or by contacting:

iUniverse
1663 Liberty Drive
Bloomington, IN 47403
www.iuniverse.com
1-800-Authors (1-800-288-4677)

ISBN: 978-1-4917-6421-3 (sc)
ISBN: 978-1-4917-6422-0 (hc)
ISBN: 978-1-4917-6423-7 (e)

Library of Congress Control Number: 2015904751

Print information available on the last page.

iUniverse rev. date: 08/14/2015

CONTENTS

INTRODUCTION

Of all events in history, few had greater consequences than the China Trade. In the 1400s, European nations thirsted for the riches of China: silk, tea, spices, and dozens of other products found nowhere else in the world. After hundreds of years of securing these items by a land route to China, Europeans began searching for a water route to China, which would be faster and less expensive. Little was known of the rest of the world and other cultures at this turning point in history.

One day in 1450, Portuguese sailors left home in search a water route to China. They bumped into Africa, traded goods for Africans, and started the practice of enslaving African people. Africans became an item of exchange in the China Trade and, as slaves, they produced products that were sold in the trade. Before slavery ended four hundred years later, the lives of thirty million Africans had been destroyed.

In 1492, Christopher Columbus began searching for a water route to China. He bumped into Haiti, and shortly thereafter European nations occupied the North and South American continents. The Natives who lived in the "New World," which wasn't new to them, were killed, conquered, or pushed aside. Before the campaign of destruction ended four hundred years later, the Native population had declined from ninety million to fewer than five million.

The European nations eventually charted a water route to China and conducted trade with the Natives of North America. The Natives who lived along the Pacific coast traded the skins of seal and otter for metal products. The trading ships sold the skins in China and used the money to buy Chinese goods. In only a few decades, the seal and otter population along the coast had declined from millions to a few thousand, and the animals were on the verge of extinction. In short, the China Trade led to the death of countless animals and of more than a hundred million people.

In spite of these deadly consequences, Europeans viewed the China Trade as a magical event full of wonder and adventure. The captains of the trading ships described fantastic voyages to Hawaii and the Spice Islands, and accounts of these places stirred the imagination of readers. There were lush tropical forests, strange new animals, long white beaches, and friendly Natives. There were new food products, bananas by the billions, and gold and silver beyond belief. Every year, some new paradise was "discovered," drawing readers deeper into the excitement of the high seas.

Although the China Trade is usually portrayed as a wonderful thing, the question that remains for all ages to ask is: Why did the China Trade lead to the death of so many people? The answer is found in the story of John Rodgers Jewitt. Like others who lived at the time, Jewitt joined the China Trade in search of adventure, but he didn't find any long white beaches or friendly Natives. Instead, he landed in a hostile world where he was forced to live as the captive of people who were very different from him. He managed to describe their world in a book called *A Narrative of the Adventures and Sufferings of John R. Jewitt*, which became the most famous account of the China Trade. Reporting on his new surroundings, Jewitt reflected the view that whites held of other cultures at the time, and this view led to the death of millions of people.

Jewitt called his new acquaintances "savages." He not only wrote that they were different, but he also described them as "degraded for their manners, morals, and customs." They were "heathens" because they had several gods and screamed at them to get the gods to obey. The Natives were "uncivilized" because they believed in revenge and killed their enemies in war. In singing to animals and offering them food, they were "childlike" and "odd," but they were more than that, according to Jewitt. They were "subhuman" because their favorite food was rotten salmon made putrid by being buried in the earth for weeks. What kind of human being would like to eat rotten fish?

Jewitt couldn't see beyond his own culture to appreciate different ways of living. Like the readers fascinated by his story, he considered other ways of life to be inferior to his own. But, in fact, the individuals he described were only savages by *his* standards. Because Jewitt's book shows prejudice toward different cultures, it helps explain why whites were so quick to enslave Africans and to push Native Americans aside. The story is a window into a time when white people considered other people inferior because they were different, and its message remains as a lesson for present and future generations.

Jewitt found out what it was like to be different, and he was not comforted by it. He was the outsider, and although he despised the "savages," he had to hide his feelings to try to fit in with them. He swallowed a meal of fish eggs floating in fat and pretended that it tasted good. He beat on the roof of a house with a stick and acted as if he understood what he was doing. He watched people pray to salmon and deer and wondered what other gods must be appeased before he could eat. He studied his "strange new world" in an attempt to understand it so he wouldn't be killed. Sad, comical, and educational, this is his story as understood today.

One

THE BOSTON

T here was little in Jewitt's background that equipped him for high adventure. He was born in 1783 in Boston, a small town on the east coast of Great Britain. Of average intelligence and stature, he had a normal childhood except he was sick more than his friends and seemed frail by comparison. Like most children at the time, Jewitt's early education occurred at home, and its focus was on the teachings of Christianity. He did receive two years of formal education, but other than learning how to read and write, he knew little beyond his own world.

Jewitt's mother died when he was three, and he was raised by a stepmother and his father, Edward, a blacksmith of considerable skill. As a young boy, Jewitt worked in his father's shop, and by the age of fourteen he had acquired the skills of a blacksmith. He might have been happy for the rest of his life working for his father and someday taking over the business, but fate intervened.

His life took a turn in 1798 when Edward moved the family to the port of Hull, north of Boston. Hull was a key link in the China Trade. It was here that ships were loaded with cargo, repaired, and made ready for the journey around the world. It was here that Jewitt learned how to repair a ship's ironwork: hinges, braces, straps, and the like. More importantly, it was here that he heard sailors' stories of exotic places and the wonders of the unknown. While working on the ships, he came to envision himself on the high seas, discovering this, exploring that, experiencing the unknown.

So when Captain John Salter of the American clipper ship the *Boston* offered to hire Jewitt as the ship's armorer (blacksmith), Jewitt eagerly accepted. With his father's approval, on September 3, 1802, he boarded the ship for an eighteen-month voyage with a crew of twenty-seven. He was only nineteen at the time. Upon his son's sailing, Edward offered some final advice: "Be honest, industrious, frugal, and temperate, and you will not fail in whatever part of the world it may be your lot to be placed."

Jewitt vomited for the first three days at sea until he acquired a tolerance for the swaying of the ship. His sickness amused the seasoned crew who knew that an armorer was important to the voyage—but this one seemed too weak for the work. He didn't walk like a sailor, and his hands seemed too small for working metal. He didn't eat like a sailor or talk like a sailor, and his face was too fine, more like the face of a schoolteacher than a blacksmith.

Once Jewitt recovered from seasickness, the crew watched him work at his forge, which was fastened to the deck. He made daggers and hatchets for trade with the Natives, and as the weapons accumulated on deck, the crew saw that Captain Salter had hired the right person for the job. They accepted Jewitt, and he became a favorite because of his friendliness and outgoing personality. One of his acquaintances was the sailmaker John Thompson, a rough, strong man. Thompson ran away to sea at the age of eight, and although he was illiterate and known mostly for brawling, the forty-year-old man got along with Jewitt as much as he got along with anyone.

From Hull, the *Boston* had a smooth voyage to Brazil, but after stopping to take on water and food, the ship battled storms as it made its way around Cape Horn at the tip of the South American continent. Jewitt became sick again. He stayed below deck and slept in a hammock—when he was able to sleep. He ate little for nearly six days, until the ship quit tossing and turning. Other crew members were sick as well, but they had to work day and night to get the ship around Cape Horn.

Once the *Boston* reached the Pacific Ocean, the sea became calm and it was an easy sail up the coast of South America. On Saturday nights, Captain Salter ordered the ship's band to play music for three hours, and the men sang about the sea and different ports of call, of which Jewitt knew nothing. During this part of the trip, several whales approached the *Boston* out of curiosity, and they fueled Jewitt's hope of adventures to come. Except for his excitement at seeing the huge whales, Jewitt, so far, found that the main features of the China Trade were work and sickness.

After seven months at sea, the *Boston* neared its destination, Vancouver Island off the coast of the Pacific Northwest. With fourteen years of experience in the China Trade, Captain Salter knew it was time to make a decision. Should he make port for supplies at Friendly Cove, located about midway up Vancouver Island, or should he continue to his final destination, Cape Scott, at the northern end of the island?

Captain John Cook was the first to charter the great island in 1778. Its waters were rich in seal and otter, and after Cook made a fortune selling skins from Vancouver, ships from other nations descended upon the region. The trade was initially centered at Friendly Cove, but by 1803, most of its marine animals had been killed, so trade was now centered at Cape Scott to the north. After considering his options, on March 12, Captain Salter steered the *Boston* into Friendly Cove for resupplying.

He didn't know that his ship was the first to enter Friendly Cove in nearly a decade. Nor could he have known how bitter the Natives were because they had been left out of the trade. No matter; his experience told him to be cautious. When Natives boarded the *Boston* to trade, the captain had them searched for weapons and personally took part in the inspections. For the next week, he traded hatchets and daggers for salmon and sent crew members ashore for timber to strengthen the masts. Meanwhile, Jewitt was the star attraction every day of the trading. Natives crowded around his forge to watch him make the weapons they so much desired, and Jewitt seemed to enjoy the attention.

On the eighth day, Chief Maquina of the Nootka boarded to oversee the final trading and see for himself how the white man on deck was making weapons. Maquina had been at the center of trading for ten years following Cook's landing. He had counseled with Cook and other captains great and small, and he knew the ways of the white man as well as any chief. They were rude and sometimes unfair in trade. They took Native women for pleasure and didn't care about people who had nothing to trade. Using a mixture of English and Indian words, Maquina quarreled with Salter over the quality of his gifts. The chief became increasingly distant.

He had other reasons for being upset. Years ago, a captain of a Spanish ship had stolen forty skins and killed four of Maquina's people. Before that, a captain of an English vessel had fired a cannon that had killed twenty of Maquina's people, including several women and children. As chief, Maquina had a long memory, and the *Boston* reminded him of what whites had previously done to his people. To ease the tension, Salter agreed to a dance on the deck of the *Boston* on the tenth and final day of trading. Jewitt knew that the chief was unhappy, but he didn't know why.

On March 22, 1803, Maquina's canoes, with a considerable number of men aboard, approached. Salter allowed them to board. Jewitt was below deck cleaning muskets when he heard a commotion on deck. Wondering what was going on, he climbed the steerage ladder, opened the hatch, and was struck on the head with an ax. The ax penetrated his skull and dropped him back, senseless. When he was awakened and escorted to deck, his vision was blurry, but he could see the figure of Maquina standing and drinking rum from a cup. The chief postponed his drinking to wrap Jewitt in Captain Salter's heavy coat.

The scene that Jewitt beheld wasn't normal for the China Trade, but it wasn't unusual either. During the dance, Maquina had positioned most of his men in a circle around the dancers; the *Boston* crew was standing in a circle just beyond. At a certain time, he gave the signal to charge, and because they had the advantage of numbers, the Natives overpowered the crew. Two crew members had been fishing on shore, and they were taken out in the well-planned attack. After the attack, the dead sailors were thrown overboard, and as far as Jewitt knew, he was the sole survivor.

Jewitt was horrified by the attack. He called it the work of "bloodthirsty savages," but Maquina's people were no worse than the whites who killed Native Americans, spread smallpox to wipe out villages, and introduced scalping to the New World. Although the massacre of the *Boston* crew was the worst thing Jewitt had seen in his life, it was a drop in the bucket compared to the bloodshed in the New World. White traders and settlers killed nine million Native Americans in what later became the United States.

To stop the bleeding, Maquina wrapped Jewitt's head with a swatch of silk—and then he poured himself another cup of rum. Unlike Jewitt and the readers of his book, Maquina was accustomed to such events and felt no remorse. His people had approved the attack to square past debts, and besides, the chief knew it wasn't the traders who were dying. It was his people who were dying at the hands of white men. As a general rule, a Native American group suffered a 90 percent collapse in population after the first hundred years of contact with whites. This wasn't Hawaii or even close to it. This was the real China Trade. For the moment, no one was talking to Jewitt, and he had no idea why his life had been spared.

In time, the sailmaker John Thompson was found hidden in a cargo hold. Natives escorted him to deck with much difficulty, as Thompson punched several in the face and kicked others after they restrained his arms. The chief was alarmed at the sight of Thompson, and Jewitt was surprised as well; but his mind was clear enough to do some fast thinking. He told Maquina that Thompson was his father and should not be killed, so the chief spared the sailmaker's life. It was a clever move, but it was hard to believe that it worked. Thompson was still ready to fight all takers, in contrast to his "son," who was passive in nature.

The business on the *Boston* was nearly finished. With a cup of rum in one hand and a dagger in the other, Maquina talked with his warriors in words that Jewitt didn't understand. Thompson was allowed rum, which he drank like water. He took more than his share in an act of defiance against the Natives who, contrary to Jewitt's account, weren't "half-naked." They were dressed in standard clothing: "kutsacks," which are robes woven of shredded bark and edged with fur. Meanwhile, Jewitt held a hand to his head and waited to see what would happen next.

Soon, a flotilla of canoes neared the *Boston*, and Maquina signaled that Jewitt should come his way. The Natives in the canoes were whooping over Maquina's victory, and those on board were yelling back, waving shirts and silk as proof of their triumph. Jewitt and Thompson were escorted into a canoe and taken ashore at Friendly Cove--captives of the Nootka Indians.

Two

SAT-SAT-SOK-SIS

As the canoes headed toward land, Jewitt hadn't a clue of who the Nootka were, other than "savages." He didn't know that they had come from Asia and settled Vancouver Island around 2500 BC, well before his own nation had been established. He had no knowledge of what it took to live on Vancouver Island for four thousand years and to survive its storms, blizzards, and freezing seas. When Caption Cook arrived in 1778, the population numbered around eighty thousand. By 1803, it was down to ten thousand, after just twenty-five years of contact with whites.

Although the circumstances weren't great, Jewitt was fortunate to experience a different way of life before it was destroyed. His first glimpse came as the canoes neared the village at Friendly Cove. The Natives had positioned themselves on the roofs and by the sides of every house, and each held a stick measuring a foot in length. When they could see the canoes, the Natives began beating on the wooden planks of the houses as fast and as hard as they could. Jewitt said the sound was "hideous, deafening, and horrible to hear, for my head still ached from the blow." But to the Nootka, it was music, and wonderful to hear. The population of the village was around twelve hundred, so Jewitt was right about one thing: the sound *was* loud.

He got a closer look as the canoes beached and Maquina jumped to shore. The drumming grew even more furious when the chief climbed up to a rooftop and other Natives began running on the beach and shouting certain words. "The savages were painted in black, save for small red squares on their faces," Jewitt said, "and their ghastly appearance, amid the infernal drumming, was a terrible sight to behold." After the canoes beached, Thompson was taken to an unknown destination, and Jewitt was led to Maquina's house.

He may have been the first white man to see the interior of a Nootka chief's home. In his book, he described it in detail. Positioned in the center of the village, the house resembled a large auditorium, but with a striking feature: a ridgepole, or beam, measuring eight feet in circumference and stretching for a hundred feet, the entire length of the roof. It was supported by massive posts at either end of the house and by three brace poles from the inside. Jewitt took note of the fact that the Nootka were skillful builders not afraid of hard work.

The roof and sides were constructed of red cedar planks, and most everything in the house was made of red cedar, the main building material available in the region. There were hundreds of mats woven from cedar bark, and baskets, buckets, and trays made from cedar. There were cedar tables, cedar chairs, cedar drums, and coils of cedar rope. Dozens of ropes hung from the rafters and held strings of dead fish suspended in air. Other ropes held the bladders of animals containing oil for cooking and lighting.

The world of the Nootka was reflected in the arrangement of the great house. More than six hundred people, about half of the village's population, slept in the house, and their quarters were assigned according to their status. Maquina slept at the far end opposite the entrance. For the others, the closer one's quarters were to the chief's, the higher in status the individual was. Accordingly, relatives slept closest to Maquina's quarters, and subchiefs, warriors, craftsmen, and the like were next in rank and assigned quarters farther away from the chief.

Although the social structure wasn't apparent to Jewitt, the Natives knew the order and knew that it wasn't fixed. A person could gain or lose status and even leapfrog to the top of the social hierarchy if he or she had done something that was of great value to the group. Nootka society was built on accomplishments that were beneficial to all, and the pecking order, so to speak, hadn't come about by accident. To survive on Vancouver Island, order was required. The Nootka emphasized status to achieve this order. Everyone worked for the good of the group, and although people weren't equal to one another, the group was orderly. Armies operate on the same the model, except promotion in rank takes longer to achieve and is awarded for different reasons.

When Jewitt entered the great house filled with people, he was immediately surrounded by women. They patted his bandaged head, as if to make it better, and stroked his face and arms in gestures of kindness. Describing the event with sarcasm, he wrote, "How sweet is compassion, even from savages!" Not knowing what else to do, he went along while trying to adjust to the odor of cedar and dead fish. It was "foul to the nose and stomach," he said, but actually it was normal and a sign of good times.

Soon the house filled with a thousand more people who had come for a feast. Using cedar trays as plates, the Nootka ate salmon, clams, sea slugs, eelgrass, and kelp. Most of the food had been cooked in or was soaking in train oil, which was liquid fat squeezed from candlefish and other marine animals. Jewitt said it was "disgusting," but, not wanting to offend Maquina, he downed a favorite Nootka meal of fish eggs floating in fat. Of all things, it didn't make him throw up.

The feast appeared to be going well until some Nootka called for Jewitt's death. Their desire to kill him arose from their concept of revenge, which Jewitt called "the strongest passion of the savage heart." But the Nootka weren't the only ones to believe in revenge. Unique to humans, revenge is as old as humanity itself and is practiced by people of most cultures. Consider, for example, "An eye for an eye and a tooth for a tooth" and "Remember Pearl Harbor!" The Nootka were only different in that they were open about their desire for revenge. They believed that the whites would retaliate because the Nootka killed some of their people aboard the *Boston*. If they killed Jewitt, the subchiefs yelled, there would be no proof of the Nootka's involvement and, hence, no payback.

Seeing an opportunity to save himself, Jewitt insisted that trade was more important to whites than settling scores. Maquina wanted to believe this, but were the whites so crazy that they would let an offense go unpunished and thereby lose their honor? Forced to choose between a core Nootkan belief and Jewitt's point, Maquina screamed that the captive should not be killed, while the subchiefs screamed that he should. Surely, Jewitt would have been better off had he not known what was being discussed. As the calls for his death continued, he suffered mental anguish to go along with the pain in his head.

Eventually, Maquina could see no way to win the argument except by force. He raised a large club and drove his people out of the house. He was strong and fast for his size, and when he caught up with stragglers, he hit them with his club. But he spared the women and children. It was clear that he would go to great lengths to keep Jewitt alive, and by now the captive knew why, thanks to the chief's explanation. His life was spared because he could make metal products.

As the chief rampaged, Jewitt capitalized on an opportunity that he thought might help him survive. One of Maquina's sons, a ten-year-old, ran to Jewitt and hugged him for reasons unknown. He hugged back, and the boy received the affection with much pleasure. Seeing a way to gain the chief's favor, Jewitt cut the buttons from Captain Salter's coat, strung them together to form a necklace, and placed the necklace around the child's neck. Highly delighted, the boy stayed at Jewitt's side, and the friendship between the two pleased Maquina.

On the following day, the Nootka looted the *Boston* and prepared it for sinking, so they could deny involvement in the slaughter if the whites came for revenge. Of course, if the whites came, then the Nootka would kill Jewitt and Thompson, which posed a major dilemma. How could they be rescued other than by a trading ship? How could they be rescued when the sight of a trading ship would lead to their murder? Jewitt would have to give this some thought, but for now, he and Thompson were made to strip the ship of its iron, which could be melted down and used for making weapons. The anvil was too heavy to move and was left behind.

During the sacking of the *Boston,* Jewitt was presented with an opportunity, and he took it. Maquina allowed him to visit Captain Salter's quarters, and when the chief wasn't looking, Jewitt took possession of a Bible and an accounting book, the pages of which were blank. Jewitt planned to fill the pages with a description of the massacre and his captivity, hoping that the journal would survive if he didn't. Thompson took a cask of rum, and when it appeared he was ready to give his life for it, the Nootka allowed him to keep it.

The booty was taken to Maquina's house, and the *Boston* was set on fire. It soon sank.

Three days after the attack on the *Boston,* scores of canoes began to arrive, and Jewitt was about to learn the extent of his importance to the Natives. Delegations from twenty tribes came to Maquina's village, some paddling two hundred miles over rough seas. They had been called for a most important ceremony, a potlatch, where the Nootka exchanged gifts and established status between the different groups. Having had little to give for nearly ten years, this was Maquina's moment to shine.

The chief was meticulous in preparing for the potlatch. Some of his people were stationed on the beach with muskets and blunderbusses (a type of musket). Others were positioned on the rooftops and at the sides of every house. Thompson appeared from nowhere and was placed behind the *Boston*'s cannon, which had been laid on planks in front of the village. With a speaking trumpet in one hand and a stick in the other, Maquina led Jewitt to the roof of the great house, and the drumming began.

As the guests arrived, they were greeted with a powerful display of bravado. Upon each new arrival, the chief let out a high, piercing sound on his trumpet, the drumming became more furious, and the muskets and blunderbusses were fired. At the same time, Thompson fired the cannon, causing the Natives to jump up and down and shout of their greatness, not unlike fans at a sporting event. Some were waving cloth and shirts as proof of victory, while others were waving daggers and hatchets. All the while—the drumming furious—Jewitt participated, his head still wrapped in silk. There he was, pounding the roof with a stick and holding a hand to his head, wishing that the "infernal racket" would stop.

That night, the great house was filled with a thousand visitors, and following a feast, there was a dance. Accompanied by drumming on planks and nearly five hundred rattles, three high-ranking chiefs danced in circles and drew white down from bags tied to their robes. As they circled, they sang in unison and scattered the feathers in the manner of falling snow. It was clear that they had performed this dance many times, as all the rattlers and drummers knew the music.

Jewitt's friend, the ten-year-old Prince Sat-sat-sok-sis, followed behind. He was adorned with small bells, and he was wearing a wolf's head. On the prince's first pass through the house, he was followed by Maquina, who was wearing a magnificent otter skin robe. He had a whistle in his mouth and a rattle in his hand to keep time to the song he was playing. After the chief sat next to Jewitt and Thompson at the head table, the prince began dancing, springing into the air from a squatting position and then turning on his heels in circles, causing the bells to jingle, which delighted the visitors. His dance lasted two hours, and each time the prince completed a swift move, the visitors chanted, "Wocash! Wocash, Tyee" ("That is good! Very good, Prince")!

At the close of the dance, Maquina conducted the potlatch, giving gifts in the name of the prince. He handed out cloth, daggers, muskets, and gunpowder. When receiving the gifts, each recipient said, "Wocash, Tyee." In return, they gave Maquina food, but it was not equal in value to the gifts they received. During the ceremony, the chief gave away one hundred muskets, four hundred yards of cloth, twenty casks of powder, and a boatload of daggers, all of which the guests carried home on the following day. The chief relished every moment of the potlatch, as did his people from outside the great house.

Jewitt could see that they were exchanging gifts, but the chief's giving away loot from the *Boston,* after going through all of the trouble of taking the ship, made no sense to him. Jewitt's people kept the spoils of war. His people established status by accumulating wealth, not by giving it away, so it wasn't surprising that he missed the point of the ceremony: to strengthen ties and ensure the well-being of all. However, he did see the importance of metal products to the potlatch and knew that his ability to make them was a way of staying alive. It was an important lesson to learn in the company of Nootka.

Three

YA-TINTLA-NO

J ewitt's friendship with Sat-sat-sok-sis resulted in another stroke of luck. It led to a relationship with Ya-tintla-no, Maquina's favorite wife and the mother of the prince. Each day, she dressed Jewitt's wound and stared down subchiefs who still wanted the captive dead. She became the caretaker of her husband's valuable possession, and she screened those who wanted to see him, such as craftsmen seeking advice and women wanting to trade. Having been taken in war, Jewitt's official status was that of a slave. But he was very lucky to be a slave here and not somewhere else.

After healing sufficiently, he was put to work on the east side of Maquina's house where he was sheltered from wind. He used a stone for an anvil and heat from a fire to shape metal. When the prince and his mother weren't around, four warriors stood guard to see that Jewitt wasn't killed. Since he wasn't ordered to make any specific product, he crafted jewelry for the Nootka, hoping to get on their good side.

He offered the first ornaments to Ya-tintla-no, who refused them and said that they should go to her son, the highest-ranking male. Once the prince received the gifts, she accepted the jewelry from him, as did Maquina's other wives. They numbered nine in total and came forward in order of their status. Afterward, onlookers approached in approximate order to receive their gifts until all the jewelry had been handed out. Early on in the giving, Jewitt knew that something was wrong because the Natives were sad and downcast. The prince and his mother appeared put down, too, which caused Jewitt to feel alarm, as he had no idea what he was doing.

As the loot from the *Boston* dwindled during other potlatches, Jewitt was ordered to make daggers and other suitable gifts. But Maquina made it clear that Jewitt was not to fall behind in repairing muskets and blunderbusses. These were also to be given away, and like the daggers, many would find their way back to Maquina during potlatches hosted by other chiefs. After observing more ceremonies, Jewitt realized that he shouldn't give a gift to someone unless the recipient had something to give back. This was why his jewelry potlatch led the Nootka to feel humiliated. This type of misunderstanding was common among crew members of ships that participated in the China Trade, as whites generally had no desire to understand the other cultures they encountered.

As a reward for his work, Jewitt was allowed to make an occasional dagger or ornament for his own use. These he traded for cloth to make shirts and pants, and for halibut and other foods suited to his tastes. Every few days, Ya-tintla-no brought fresh salmon, and Jewitt reciprocated by giving her son an item acquired in trade, a button, a ball of string, or a swatch of silk. He made sure that his gifts were of lower value than the salmon, which showed respect. In addition, participating in these exchanges strengthened his position in the group. He slept in the great house next to the prince, barely five feet from the chief's quarters.

But Jewitt was only role-playing. While exchanging gifts, he secretly believed that the Nootka's rules for giving were "foolish." While exercising his metalworking skills to keep his rank elevated, he secretly believed that the Nootkas' concern about status was "a characteristic of primitive people." And every night he prayed for deliverance from "the ignorant savages of this barbaric land."

By contrast, Thompson lived in open disgust of the Nootka—and there were more like him in the China Trade than Jewitt. He was given heavy work dragging chunks of cedar to the village, but he barely followed orders. Unconcerned with the status of any Nootka, he shoved them when they were in his way. He even showed defiance of Maquina, cursing him and walking away while the chief was talking. Whenever the chief saw Thompson, he said, "John, you die—Thompson kill." Thompson would just stare back and dare the chief to kill him. Jewitt shared food with Thompson, who slept in the great house wherever there was a space. The Natives considered him ignorant and impolite. Thompson's position was, *What are you going to do about it?*

After two months in captivity, it appeared that the whites weren't coming after all, and so the calls for Jewitt's death died down. His guards were dismissed. He had moments of freedom and had learned enough Nootka words to know what was being said in the tribal council. Knowing something about what was going on, he felt more secure, and so the time seemed right to start his journal. If he died in captivity but his journal survived, then Maquina would pay for the massacre of the *Boston*'s crew. So Jewitt believed in revenge, too.

While walking the shoreline, he collected crows' quills to use as writing pens. In his trips to the woods, he experimented with plants to perfect the ingredients for making ink. Thompson offered his own blood for use as ink, and he was dead serious about it. Instead, Jewitt mixed the juice of blackberries with charcoal, boiled the liquid, then filtered it through cloth. He preserved the ink in bottles acquired through trade and started writing for brief periods of time when he was alone in the woods.

In one of the great ironies of the China Trade, Maquina's tolerance for other people's religion gave Jewitt time to write about "savages." By the start of the summer, he had told the chief that he and Thompson were Christians and that Sunday was their holy day when they needed to pray alone. It struck Maquina as strange, because Nootka religion was tied to seasons, not to a specific day of the week. But he understood the need for prayer and so granted the request. Weather permitting, Jewitt and Thompson retired every Sunday to a pond about a mile from the village.

It was the most enjoyable day of the week during Jewitt's captivity, because on Sunday he could be himself. After the two men bathed and changed into clean clothes, Thompson sat by the shore while Jewitt stood and read aloud from the Bible. The Scripture reading was followed by a hymn Jewitt sung alone, and the hymn was followed by a prayer from the *Book of Common Prayer*, which was among those items Jewitt had taken from Captain Salter's quarters. He ended each service by asking God to rescue them from the savages, and then he wrote in his journal. All the while, Thompson slept under a tree near his stash of rum. The Nootka would have thought these activities dull, and maybe comical, but they didn't consider it any of their business.

After describing the attack on the *Boston*, potlatches, and the like in his journal, Jewitt focused on Thompson's most recent behavior. Jewitt was doing some work for a subchief when a courier brought word that Maquina was about to kill Thompson. Jewitt rushed to the chief's house and found Maquina face-to-face with Thompson, pointing a musket at his chest. Thompson stood defiantly, baring his chest and daring Maquina to fire, while Jewitt hurried to find a solution to whatever the problem was.

Details aside, the problem was Thompson. On this occasion, some boys had teased Thompson and he struck their leader, Sat-sat-sok-sis. Thompson knew who the boy was and also knew that he risked death by hitting Sat-sat-sok-sis, but as Jewitt wrote, "He would take nothing from the savages, even at my insistence that he act in a less offensive way." Two weeks later, Thompson hit Maquina's oldest son, who was eighteen. He knocked him down, bloodied his face, and kicked him in the sides.

In both cases, Jewitt saved Thompson's life by lying. He told Maquina that if his father were killed, he would take his own life. Although suicide was against Jewitt's religion, Maquina didn't know this, and so he believed Jewitt's threat. Accordingly, he ordered his people to stay clear of Thompson, but the chief kept reminding him that the debt would be squared: "John, you die—Thompson kill." It wasn't possible for Jewitt to go back to the deck of the *Boston* and have a talk with the sailmaker about survival techniques. It wouldn't have helped anyway. Thompson was Thompson. Because Jewitt had lied while on the deck of the *Boston,* saying that Thompson was his father, he had only himself to blame for the headache that was John Thompson.

Fortunately, though, Jewitt wrote about what he saw. During the summer months, he described the ways in which the Natives secured food. Since the rugged terrain of the island made farming impossible, the Nootka had to collect enough food for twelve hundred people to eat over the next six months. Jewitt described the food gathering in neutral terms, much like a scientist would, and although his descriptions are highly informative, he missed the wonder of people surviving in what he himself called "a godforsaken land."

After thousands of years of observation, the Nootka had become experts on nature, and the intelligence they exhibited in obtaining food was equal to that required for planting seeds and harvesting crops. In the inlets of Friendly Cove, the Nootka submerged tree branches in ten feet of water and anchored them with rocks so herring would lay their eggs on the ready-made nests. Off shore, in the ocean, they caught halibut, salmon, cod, and tuna by carefully positioning dozens of canoes and then charging at the fish full-speed. They drove the fish into cedar-bark nets that stretched for two hundred feet. They also had an ingenious way of catching individual salmon—by using a hook attached to a paddle. As the paddler rowed, the salmon struck the moving bait, and with one motion of the paddle, the fisherman flung the salmon into the canoe.

Smelt, sprat, and the prized candlefish were caught in nets. Seal, otter, porpoises, and sea lions were taken after impaling themselves on stakes that had been planted in seaweed. Men dove in the ocean for starfish and clams, women worked reefs for barnacles and plants, and children chased crabs on the beach. They filled hundreds of buckets with mussels, urchins, anemones, kelp, barracuda, herring, sea bass, and octopus. The liquid fat from candlefish, called train oil, was poured over the food to preserve it and season it to Nootka taste.

They ate what was available and acquired a taste for most everything, because salmon might be scarce one year and berries the next. This kept their diet healthy. In addition, changes in the natural world continually led them to upgrade their knowledge of nature. They took note of a fire that was destined to wipe out a grazing area. They made note of an unusual tide that might affect a salmon run. And they didn't need to write down this information in some book on nature. It was fixed in the minds of the Nootka, which weren't cluttered with useless information and impermanent truths. Time-tested for four thousand years, the theory behind Nootka food-gathering practices was based on what they could see and what they knew to be true. Otherwise, they were finished.

Jewitt might have been more impressed with the food gathering had he been asked to secure three tuna and a quart of herring spawn. He took food for granted, as he had all his life, and didn't fully appreciate its value to the Nootka. Besides having to endure the lean times they faced every year, the Nootka also held many ceremonies in the winter months, for which Maquina's people needed extra food to give away to maintain the chief's status. Also, his rivals needed food to give away so they could receive. To Jewitt, the food gathering seemed like something the Nootka just did. But to them, it was a pledge for the survival of all. Luckily, *all* included Jewitt, who survived because the Nootka shared food with him.

In the course of food gathering, Jewitt learned how the Natives celebrated a special event, such as one of Maquina's wives giving birth to a son. They held a feast that was comparable to Jewitt's eating in the finest restaurant in the world. After burying salmon in the ground for months to rot, the Nootka strung the fish from houses for two weeks, until the sun further putrefied the meat. The odor extended for miles, and Jewitt couldn't escape it, even at the pond. He said it was "the foulest stench imaginable, wretched, horrid, and impossible to bear," but it wasn't to the Nootka. Salmon prepared this way was such a delicacy that they never offered Jewitt a share, which was another break for him during his captivity.

This was his summer routine, describing food gathering and rotting fish, until Jewitt was caught writing in his journal. Because he never thought he would get caught, Jewitt had no ready explanation other than to say he was writing about the weather. Maquina didn't believe him and was certain that the captive was writing about the *Boston*—and that whites would come for revenge. He was so mad at the captive that he beat Jewitt with a stick until he was covered in welts and fell to the ground. The tribal council called for Jewitt's death, and Jewitt prepared to say his final prayers.

Ya-tintla-no saved Jewitt's life and, incidentally, Thompson's. She argued that the prince would never forget who killed his best friend and that he would avenge Jewitt's death by killing the chief, which would mean the end of the village. Ya-tintla-no was a woman of great beauty and intelligence, and she knew that her husband always put his people first. The idea that the whole tribe would be lost without a chief led the chief to spare the captives. With Sat-sat-sok-sis at his mother's side and Maquina still looking angry, Jewitt knelt before the chief and promised he would never write in the book again. In this case, the threat of revenge saved Jewitt's life.

The beating Jewitt received worsened the pain in his head. In addition, he suffered psychological terror, knowing that he might be killed at any moment for one reason or another: if Maquina was seriously challenged by subchiefs and Jewitt was the issue; if Sat-sat-sok-sis or Ya-tintla-no turned against him; if he ran out of metal and couldn't make gifts; if Thompson pushed Maquina too far; or if a ship showed up in Friendly Cove. But death would be instantaneous if he was caught writing a second time. Maquina told him that.

Four

TASHEES

The need for prayer at Friendly Cove was evident when the first autumn storm arrived, a four-hour pounding of wind and rain. At the storm's onset, people rushed to the roofs and to the sides of houses, and the drumming began. Illuminated by crackling lightning, Maquina stood on the peak of the great house and sang to Quahootze, the Supreme Being who controlled other gods. He sang and the villagers drummed until Quahootze heard the prayer and stopped the storm.

Jewitt experienced the prayer from inside the great house, where the pain in his head set a new record. By now, the house was splendidly Nootka and smelled of success. There were boxes stacked ten feet high containing more than a hundred different foods. There were buckets overflowing with eelgrass and trunks packed with salmon. There was hardly any room left on the rafters to hang bladders and fish. For the past two weeks, the food had been under guard twenty-four hours a day, and the guards did not leave to take part in the prayer to Quahootze. Jewitt was confused about the new situation. The house was a grocery store of food, but little of it was being eaten.

The last two weeks of summer was a difficult time for the village because during this period the Nootka lived near to starvation to ensure that food would be available during the winter. Jewitt and Thompson were allowed no more than the others, and the Nootka refused to share food. Even Ya-tintla-no and the prince hoarded their shares, leaving Jewitt with the impression that Nootka society had completely broken down. What about gift giving? What about favors from friends in high places? What about order? Every family seemed to be on its own.

Knowing that Maquina would never interrupt someone's holy day, Jewitt kept writing every Sunday at the pond. During the lean time, he said that the Natives had "sad faces," were "withdrawn," and had become "a different people." It wasn't true. Their sacrifice was still for the good of their group, and it was also to ensure the survival of outside groups. As for the soldiers guarding the food, they were necessary because some subchiefs weren't above stealing food to stop the grumbling in their stomachs. The guards were proof that all societies have flaws.

The first storm hit on September 2. Once the sky cleared, Jewitt was told that he had two days to pack his belongings because the tribe was moving. That was the amount of time it took to disassemble a Nootka village—that is, take apart a whole community and relocate it. Perplexed, Jewitt watched as the plank boards were removed from the roof and sides of the great house until all that remained was the ridgepole, brace poles, and outside frame. All the boards from the other houses were removed as well, and the village came to look like the remains of a vanquished people. The planks were long and heavy, and Thompson was asked to carry a portion, knowing that he liked any work that required muscle. Jewitt was watching until he was told to start carrying food, which he did with help from Thompson.

The boxes of this and bowls of that, the cedar this and cedar that, were loaded into canoes that spanned the entire length of Friendly Cove. Men of high status untied the ropes from the rafters and carried the bladders to shore, and families carried their own possessions as well as the possessions of others: tables, chairs, mats, drums, bowls, stools, coils of rope, bows and arrows, kutsacks, rattles, diapers made of rabbit fur, and drumming sticks. Thompson moved the cannon while Jewitt packed his stuff—after hiding his journal on his person. More than eighty canoes were loaded with people and possessions, and just like that, the Nootka were out of there.

As the boats pushed off at Friendly Cove, Jewitt had a sinking feeling. He had lost his understanding of the Natives, such as it was, and wondered if they would ever again share with him and be friendly. Adding to his depression was the thought of leaving Friendly Cove. In spite of its strong winds and bad odor, it was a sanctuary where he had found some peace. Now it was gone, along with the pond and, probably, any chance of his rescue. He did not know that his chances for rescue were already slim. Word of the massacre of the *Boston* crew had spread along the coast, so trading ships now avoided Friendly Cove at all costs.

The canoes proceeded north into a narrow inlet between Nootka Island and Vancouver Island. Maquina led the way, and the others followed behind in a line of boats that stretched for nearly a mile. Loaded to the brim with cargo, the boats cleared the surface of the water by mere inches. Paddlers struggled against the strong current.

There was a guide at the bow of each canoe, and he gave orders to go right and left to avoid jagged reefs and trees that had been toppled by storms and now littered the river. There was no place to land a boat if a storm hit with high winds, and there was no stopping for lunch or rest; the trip had to be completed in one day because of the chance of storm. By late afternoon, the canoes reached a deep bay, and from there, the Nootka paddled up a river to Maquina's autumn village at Tashees, where storms were less severe.

Tashees resembled the village at Friendly Cove when the Nootka left—and the people reconstructed their village in two days on this new site. Maquina's ridgepole was shorter, about eighty feet, and the houses were closer together, as the site was small and compact. "I could hear banging and clatter in the woods for weeks," Jewitt wrote. What he heard were the noises of other groups assembling their villages, positioning planks on the roofs and sides of their houses, and carrying possessions from the beach. There were twenty-five villages, and they were all within a few miles of Maquina's group.

Unfortunately for Jewitt, with each storm came a prayer, and all the Nootka in all the villages—some ten thousand people— drummed all at once. There was no escaping the prayers, even on Sunday when Jewitt and Thompson were in the woods trying to reach their God, or at least Jewitt was. The prayers—or, as he put it, "the infernal drumming of the savages"—made it hard for Jewitt to hear his own prayers, never mind sleep. For his own sake, he might have prayed for the storms to end so that the drumming would stop, or he might have joined the Nootka and helped make the prayer louder so Quahootze could hear it. Either approach was better than complaining about the way others worshipped.

At Tashees, Jewitt was allowed to travel with Maquina and see the chief receive gifts from other villages. These were occasions when the chief's humanity shone through, although it wasn't Jewitt's intention to present Maquina in a positive light. The chief wore a fine otter robe and a conical hat edged with fur. He danced and spread down. He rattled and whistled. From behind a duck mask, he sang to his host and to Ya-tintla-no, who was dressed in her best robe and rattling with both hands. Afterward, Maquina gave salmon and received daggers, saying, "Wocash, Tyee." Jewitt never said exactly when the Nootka snapped out of their gloom, but it was clear that they were back to normal at the first potlatch Maquina hosted.

With Tashees came new work assignments. Jewitt was told to make fishhooks. These figured into nearly every potlatch, as tribes low on food needed hooks to fish for salmon in between storms. Thompson was enlisted for equally important work, which Jewitt described with more passion than he did food gathering.

The logs that Thompson hauled at Friendly Cove were used to make tables, drums, and the like. At Tashees, he hauled logs that the Nootka fashioned into canoes for fishing and for reaching Tashees in order to survive, which was still important to Jewitt, if not to Thompson. Only the autumn months provided time for canoe making. It took three months to make a canoe from a tree, and people's lives depended on the work being done right.

The process started with two days of singing, fasting, and praying. The Natives worked in groups of ten, and as they sat in a circle and sang, their heads were adorned with down so that they would be blessed. After fasting and praying, the groups entered the forest and sang to the woodpecker, the guardian spirit of the forest. Hours of singing and looking at trees were required to find the one that had been chosen by the woodpecker. It was as large and straight as Maquina's ridgepole and showed clear evidence of having been pecked.

Once found, the tree was set on fire at its base, and clay was added above to stop the fire from spreading; eventually, the tree hit the ground with a crash. After removing the bark and branches, the men shortened the log to fifty feet, with a uniform circumference of eight feet. They then rolled the log into a river that ran near the village, with some of the workers jumping into the water to act as guides. Where there was no river, people dragged the log to the village, with Thompson at the lead rope, pulling like a plow horse.

Workers used chisels to hollow the log, which created mounds of wood chips and sent them flying in every direction. Afterward, the workers filled the log with water and added hot stones to keep the water boiling for two days so as to cure the wood and seal it tight. Once the log was emptied, men inserted cedar spreaders to widen it. These spreaders were left in to serve as seats, and once the log was widened, the front and back of the canoe were narrowed, a splashboard was added, and the bottom and sides were sanded with dogfish and then with sharkskin to make the wood smooth for cutting through water. The canoe was finished when the figure of a duck's head was added to the bow and workers offered a final prayer. Jewitt said that the Nootka built five canoes ranging from thirty to fifty feet in length. He wrote that the work "required much patience and skill," but said little about the role of prayer.

Jewitt's other writings at Tashees focused on Maquina and the growing friendship between himself and the chief. Thinking that Jewitt had kept his word and wasn't writing in his journal anymore, Maquina had several conversations with Jewitt, including one where the chief detailed the grievances that led him to take the *Boston*, namely that whites had killed his people, stolen skins from him, and abused his women. The two men fished together, and the chief took Jewitt hunting. Jewitt shot two ducks to Maquina's six. While on one particular outing, Jewitt witnessed another event that was core to being Nootka.

In December, he accompanied Maquina to check traps that had been set for bears. These were situated on the banks of a river where salmon spawned and bears came to eat. Made from cedar boards, the traps stood six feet high and were like little houses, except the door was only large enough for the head of a bear—and the roof sagged from the weight of boulders. Poking its head in, the bear tugged on a string of salmon fastened to a trip plank on the roof, and the boulders came crashing down. Two bears were taken in December, much to the chief's delight.

In each case, the bear was washed in the river and its fur dried and combed. Then it was carried to Maquina's house, which was jammed with visitors for the important event. The animal was seated upright in a chair and was adorned with Maquina's best bonnet. As guests watched, Maquina sprinkled eagle feathers on the bear and said, "We have waited for you to visit us for a long time. Here is the eagle down you came to get." He placed a tray of food on the bear's lap and invited it to eat, saying, "Hah-welks moo-watch" ("Hungry bear"). While the bear was being prepared to be eaten, Sat-sat-sok-sis danced for two hours. Then the meat was offered to guests.

At the first feast, no one ate the bear. At the second, only ten people accepted trays, while the rest ate salmon and crabs. Jewitt and Thompson refused the meat after Maquina explained that anyone eating bear meat would be prohibited from eating meat or fish for the next two months to atone for disgracing the bear. The ten people who ate bear at the second feast lived on berries and roots for the next two months, but that was not what confounded Jewitt. If the bear was so sacred to the Nootka, he wondered, then why did they kill it in the first place? The answer is that they killed it in order to show respect. All animals were considered sacred, and bears ranked near the top. The Nootka honored all animals by offering food to the bear and by refusing to eat its meat. It had to be killed for this to take place. It wasn't like present-day Thanksgiving where someone else kills the turkey, but the principle was the same: giving thanks for one's food.

The most important event at Tashees was the tribute to Quahootze, which Jewitt wasn't allowed to see. All he knew was that it involved every village drumming as loudly as possible. On December 13, the Nootka turned "hysterical," he said, and Maquina ordered the captives to go into the woods and not return for fourteen days. They went into the forest and lived in a hut made of branches and mud and were kept alive by Thompson's fire and by food brought by Ya-tintla-no. Although cold and often hungry, Jewitt had a bigger problem, which led to another sinking feeling.

Just days before he was banished, Jewitt had gone back to thinking that his death was imminent. This time, the issue was his apparent value to other groups. Maquina's rivals were jealous of his advantage, and during ceremonies they invited Jewitt to live with them, saying that he would have a better life there and that they would benefit by giving away the metal products he made. Upon hearing of the offers, Maquina flew into a rage and told the captive that he would have him killed if he tried to leave. Jewitt said that he would never leave the village and go to live with unknown people in unknown places, but that neither stopped the offers nor calmed Maquina. Now when the chief said, "John, you die," he didn't mean Thompson.

While the Nootka were honoring Quahootze, Jewitt prayed that he wouldn't be killed. In the freezing hut at Tashees, he asked to be delivered "from the savages, who have no notion of God, but, instead, spend hours and days drumming with sticks and singing." The drumming gave Thompson a headache, and Jewitt wrote that the sailmaker "vowed to end their degraded race and wished he had the means to do so." After two weeks, the drumming stopped, and the two men were allowed to return to the village. Jewitt was thankful and believed that God had heard his prayer. Thompson was too embittered to think of anything other than killing his tormentors.

Five

COOPTEE

O
n December 30, when the captives returned to the village, the first snow fell on Tashees, and the Nootka began making preparations to vacate the site. Knowing the routine, Jewitt carried food, Thompson hauled planks, and the two helped Ya-tintla-no with her possessions. The villagers headed back down the inlet between Vancouver Island and Nootka Island, the canoes plowing through sheets of ice that had recently formed. Although bundled in Captain Salter's coat, Jewitt was cold, but he was happy to have a break from the offers to buy him. He was also gloomy and withdrawn. After the tribute to Quahootze, the Nootka became gloomy and withdrawn again, and Jewitt adopted their attitude.

It took fourteen hours to reach Nootka Sound and paddle up a river to Cooptee, the site of Maquina's winter village. The people reassembled the village in two days. After they finished the job, they sat around fires and showed disinterest in everything, including eating. Soon, scouts returned from an upstream expedition, and the great house became alive with conversation and eating. Quahootze had filled the river with herring, so the Nootka's disinterest in his doing so was no longer required. The apparent disinterest wasn't what it appeared to be. It was like silence during a prayer. Unknowingly, Jewitt had prayed to Quahootze by being silent and withdrawn.

During the winter months, blizzards prevented the Nootka from holding a number of ceremonies, so social status remained fixed for a time. When a tribe could manage a potlatch, food was the main item of exchange, so Jewitt was now less important to Maquina's rivals. However, Cooptee was a tough place for an outsider to be. On Sundays in the forest, Jewitt constantly complained about his numb hands and feet and his ears that ached from the cold. The Natives didn't seem bothered by the cold and went about their business as usual. At Cooptee, that meant fishing for herring. Jewitt accepted just one invitation to go on a fishing expedition as an observer.

It wasn't easy to catch herring because they swim in schools and spook easily. The Nootka solved this problem by engineering special paddles that enabled them to move across the water in near silence. The blades were thin so they could enter water without a splash, and they were tapered at the tip so water ran off them quickly and quietly. There were eight paddlers in Jewitt's canoe, which he estimated to be forty feet long. It was cold and snowing hard when the boat came upon the first school.

Because herring couldn't be caught with nets or hooks, the Nootka made a special tool for taking the fish. It was a long stick, the last two feet of which had been flattened to two inches in width and fitted with eels' teeth. Maquina and three others were at the bow, holding the sticks high in the air as they moved over the fish. Jewitt characterized the assault as "furious and unrelenting." The men hammered the sticks into the water and then slung them back into the canoe, shaking the herring loose. Each man snagged about ten fish per blow and thrashed the water up to thirty times within the space of two minutes before the fish were gone. An average assault netted close to a thousand fish, but on this trip, with three other canoes out, the total catch was four thousand herring in two minutes.

For the second time in his captivity, Jewitt conceded that the Natives were to be admired for something besides canoe making. He wrote, "The snow made it hard to see, but the chief found the schools of fish throughout the day. At every stop, the fish were flung into the boat until we were knee-deep in fish and I was covered in snow and suffering in pain from the cold. To fish under such conditions," he concluded, "required much endurance and ingenuity." But to the Nootka, it was just another day at Cooptee. As they headed back to the village, they sang to the fish and offered thanks to Quahootze.

After the fishing trip, Maquina took Jewitt to another village situated like Cooptee. When the canoes pushed off at midmorning, Jewitt didn't know the reason for the trip, but the absence of salmon and other gifts indicated that his group wasn't going for a potlatch. There were eight boats carrying subchiefs, warriors, women, and children, and the trip took two hours through moderate to heavy snows. All Jewitt knew was that they were going to another village and that he should not speak until Maquina gave him permission.

Upon entering the chief's house, Maquina and his people began socializing and left Jewitt to the mercy of a crowd that was "rude and ill-mannered," he said. The Natives in this village hadn't been involved in the China Trade, and some had never seen a white man. They were curious about the visitor's clothing and pulled on Captain Salter's coat. They poked Jewitt's arms and feet and opened his mouth to see if he had a tongue. "I-yee ma hak" ("I do not understand"), they murmured, "I-yee ma hak." They were startled to see such a weird creature and wondered if he was human.

After some time, Maquina told Jewitt to speak, and when he did, his words revealed that he was not only human but also extremely ill-mannered. Why was he wearing a blue coat and trousers if not to mock the seal? What kind of person would mimic the seal and risk being denied its meat? He was urged to remove the clothing while Maquina looked on in apparent amusement. "Wik, cham-mas-sish" ("No, pleasant to the taste"), Jewitt said, which was all he could come up with at the time. It was a case of a guest disrespecting his host. The Nootka felt shame, although from their point of view, they weren't the ones who were "rude and ill-mannered." Eventually, Maquina rescued Jewitt and sat him at a table, while children played and people talked of common interests.

The subject of conversation at the table was the weather, food, and sickness, and who was ill and in which village and why. Although Maquina's hosts hadn't had contact with whites, white sailors spread sexually transmitted diseases to the village, and people had died from these diseases, as they had in other villages. The talk led Maquina to the *Boston*. As he described the attack, he glared at Jewitt and directed remarks his way. It was clear that the chief hated the sailors for raping his women. It was also clear that he was frustrated because revenge was impossible. The sailors had abused so many women that Maquina couldn't imagine how the debt could be squared. And because it couldn't be squared, the offense could never be forgotten.

The socializing lasted well into the afternoon. There was no potlatch, and the only food brought to the table was herring eggs, which Jewitt had come to tolerate. Most of the families were sitting on mats and talking when Maquina left the table and moved among them. He walked slowly and alternated between talking and singing. He dropped down when he sang, and he touched the shoulders of the sons of his host. Jewitt watched from the table while helping Sat-sat-sok-sis with the toys he had traded for—miniature boats and carved figurines of deer and elk. That was all there was to the trip.

Although his presence was important to Maquina—probably to show him off—the captive was a bit player in the socializing at Cooptee.

Sometime after returning to the village, Jewitt became entangled in the ordeal of Tootoosch, who was a high-ranking chief. Tootoosch was the husband of one of Maquina's sisters, and his problem stretched all the way back to the *Boston*. He had killed the two crew members who had been fishing on shore, John Hall and Samuel Wood. Four days after he killed Hall and Wood, Tootoosch's oldest daughter died mysteriously. The chief became depressed, and as the group was leaving Tashees for Cooptee, Tootoosch said that he was being haunted by the ghosts of Hall and Wood. They were standing next to him and wouldn't let him eat.

Subchiefs forced food into his mouth to keep him alive, but his problem only got worse. After six weeks at Cooptee, Tootoosch's only son and only tyee, an eleven-year-old, died mysteriously. The chief went insane, and he became the focus of the village. Was this how the whites were coming for revenge—through the ghosts of the *Boston* crew? The answer wasn't clear, but it was believed that Jewitt and Thompson might have summoned the ghosts of Hall and Wood. The subchiefs called for the captives' death, again; the tribal council agreed, again; Maquina said no, but the village stood against him. Club in hand, he drove his people out of the great house, again.

The arguing went on for weeks until both sides agreed to ask Tootoosch if the captives were responsible for his madness. They made the trip to see him under guard. Their departure was accompanied by drumming from the rooftops, which were edged with icicles, as by now it was very cold. In this instance, Jewitt knew that he couldn't catch a break and that his life depended on what Tootoosch said, if his words could be understood at all. When Maquina led the group in, Tootoosch was flailing his arms and yelling, "Hall, peshak;

Wood, peshak" ("Hall, bad; Wood, bad"). When the chief asked if the captives were responsible, Tootoosch said, "Wik! Wik!" ("No! No!"), much to Jewitt's relief. Tugging on Jewitt's sleeve, Tootoosch offered him food, saying, "John klushish" ("John is good").

Tootoosch didn't seem all that mad, so Jewitt tried to convince him that Hall and Wood weren't present. Waving his arms and holding his eyes shut, the chief replied that he knew that while others couldn't see the men, they were present and wouldn't leave him alone. Searching for a solution, Maquina asked Jewitt how his people cured such illnesses, and Jewitt answered that the deranged were whipped. Accordingly, Maquina secured a branch and ordered Tootoosch whipped—by Thompson. It was the first time Thompson seemed happy among the Nootka. He whipped Tootoosch for nearly an hour, until Maquina determined that it wasn't working and ordered that he stop. Tootoosch's madness continued.

In the end, it helped Jewitt stay alive. The villagers believed that Hall and Wood were present because they could see the effect on Tootoosch. As a result, the council voted not to kill the captives so that their ghosts wouldn't return to haunt any of their people. Although this was the reason why Jewitt was still alive, he believed that Tootoosch's madness was a gift from God. "The intervention of an all-merciful God," he wrote, "permitted the spirits of the dead to revisit the world and haunt the barbarians to respect our lives." So Jewitt believed in ghosts, too.

Jewitt wrote about Tootoosch in a frozen hut at Cooptee. This time, his banishment lasted for three weeks, but he couldn't determine the purpose. When he asked Ya-tintla-no to explain it, she said, "Tar-toose, Noowexa" ("Stars, Father" or "Stars for Father"), which made no sense and may have been intended to make no sense. If Jewitt was right in thinking that Ya-tintla-to was behind his banishment, then it is possible that she may have kept the reason to herself, for his sake. It probably had something to do with preventing his death. She brought herring every day and was finally smiling when she signaled that Jewitt and Thompson should come and rejoin the others.

The two had been called back for a feast that Jewitt called "sinful" without ever trying to understand its purpose. Maquina's house was packed with visitors, including people from the village whom Jewitt had visited and offended. He wrote that all the Natives did for three days was eat. They stuffed themselves with putrefied salmon that had been saved for the occasion and poured double servings of train oil onto every meal, until all animal bladders were empty and all stomachs bulging. Jewitt said the food was "squandered by a gluttonous people" and that the feast was "an affront to the Provider." It was not. It was a display of faith. When the Nootka returned to Friendly Cove, Quahootze would see that they had no food and would replenish the sea. By now, Jewitt should have known that anything he didn't understand probably had to do with Nootka religion.

Soon after the feast, Jewitt was on his knees, praying in the snow of Cooptee and preparing for death once again. On February 23, a courier brought word that twenty ships were on their way to Friendly Cove to kill the people responsible for the *Boston*. The news threw Maquina into a rage because he was conflicted. On the one hand, he had to kill the captives before returning to Friendly Cove. On the other hand, if he killed them, then their ghosts might return to haunt his people. The chief hurled boxes inside the great house and destroyed Jewitt's workplace. Then word arrived that the report of the ship sightings might be a hoax perpetrated by Maquina's enemies. With this, the chief became more upset because he didn't know what to believe. His display of anger and frustration spread throughout the village. In packing for Friendly Cove, the Nootka hurled boards into canoes, pitched in rattles, and slammed boxes against one another.

As he did with most things Nootka, Jewitt disparaged Maquina's people for "acting as one," as if they should have been fighting among themselves instead. Like a nation at war or grieving for a fallen leader, the Nootka were bound together by strong emotions of loyalty. What should they have done—ignore their leader and his crisis? Conversely, Maquina was in turmoil because the fate of his people was at stake. What should he have done—ignore the fate of his people?

As he said his final prayers, Jewitt didn't know which way Maquina would go. For nearly a year, his life had seemed like science fiction, with wild shifts from safety to certain death. Earlier that morning, he wrote what he thought might be the last entry in his journal: "Nothing could be more unpleasant than our present situation. Our lives are entirely dependent on the will of a savage, on whose whims and suspicions no rational calculation can be made. Upon our death, may God claim our souls."

Because Jewitt was still valuable to the group, Maquina wanted to believe that the report of the ships was a hoax. Therefore, he acted rationally. For the moment, the captives were spared, but they were treated as outcasts during the trip to Friendly Cove. The chief was in the lead boat with his wives and children. Tootoosch was with some subchiefs and most of the weapons. Jewitt and Thompson were with warriors who had instructions to kill the captives at the first sign of whites. Jewitt's eyes were fixed on the horizon as the canoes moved closer and closer to the place where his adventure had begun.

Six

MAH-HACK

There were no ships at Friendly Cove when the Nootka arrived. Jewitt rejoiced inside but remained cautious because he knew his future was still uncertain. Maquina kept watching for the ships, and Jewitt kept studying the chief's mood. Then, after two weeks, Maquina concluded that he had been the victim of a hoax, so he dismissed the warriors who were guarding the captives. Once again, Jewitt thanked God for his life. On his first Sunday back at the pond, he sang hymn solos and wrote that he was glad to be "home." It was as though he needed a sense of belonging, but not so for Thompson, who was back to staring down the Nootka for being pushy.

After catching up in his journal, writing about the last weeks at Cooptee, Jewitt described everyday life in the village. His account includes specialists making paddles, women weaving mats, and children competing in running contests and target practice with bow and arrow. Whether working or relaxed, the adults were talkative and enjoyed teasing each other if one made a drum that was off pitch or a bowl that tilted sideways. One journal entry related that the canoe maker Utootoo had risen in status after his work at Tashees. Another said that Prince Lat-lat-sac had lost favor because of a mishap while hunting. Jewitt still had trouble understanding the Nootka, but he could describe them without judging them, if he tried.

This style of plain description was hard to maintain when writing about the ceremonies at Friendly Cove, which he had either missed the year before or else hadn't bothered to record. Because he wasn't Nootka and didn't understand why they believed as they did, he said that their ceremonies were based on "superstitions." But he would find it hard to explain why his fellow Europeans felt that the number thirteen should be avoided and that a person shouldn't cross the path of a black cat.

Because salmon were so important to the Nootka diet, it was crucial that Maquina perform the salmon ceremony correctly, so the fish would return to Friendly Cove. On the first day of the ceremony, a canoe left the village at midafternoon and carried the chief some seventy miles from the ocean's shore. In darkness and with no land in sight, he slipped into the cold water and began swimming toward his village, while other chiefs swam toward their villages. A rope was tied around his neck, and as he swam, he towed shells and starfish that called the salmon to come. He swam until he was exhausted, and the next night he picked up where he had left off. He reached the village on the seventh night, as the ceremony required, and although he was weak and cold, he had demonstrated once again that his people were worthy of the fish.

The fish came a few days later as visitors. They numbered around twenty, but only one was taken. After covering the fish with feathers, the villagers began a three-day fast. A shaman (a religious figure) prepared the fish for eating, while others sang to the fish and praised its qualities, saying "Wocash so-har" and "Katlahtik so-har" ("Good salmon" and "Brother salmon"). It was eaten by the entire village—an accomplishment in itself—and the skeleton was returned to the water to hail others to come.

Another ceremony involved bathing in the streams of Nootka Island. People did this every morning and every evening for four days, until the village was cleansed and ready to receive any gifts that might be offered. Spring was the time of renewal, when a person might acquire the ability to hunt a certain animal or lay branches correctly so herring would use them to spawn.

To aid in receiving, the Nootka swallowed a liquid that made them vomit. It was the only thing that made them vomit, Jewitt remarked. By rendering themselves empty, they showed a willingness to receive and displayed respect for the spiritual forces that controlled animals. Quahootze was above these spirits, which were like angels, but unlike Quahootze, the spirits couldn't be ordered to obey. They required that the Nootka fast and cleanse their bodies before they could eat. Although more elaborate in detail, the ceremonies served the same purpose as a family prayer before dinner or a fast for a prescribed period.

Shortly after March 22, 1804, at the one-year mark of his captivity, Jewitt's attitude toward the Nootka completely flip-flopped. He stopped criticizing them for praying to false gods, engaging in gluttonous behavior, and acting as one, and he became captivated by a key element of their culture. He had missed it the year before because he had been under guard and confined to his workplace. But since Tashees, he had been wondering what Maquina's purpose was in performing a certain ceremony over and over. Now Jewitt found out.

At the first waxing of the moon in November, when the moon appeared in a crescent shape, the chief entered the river in front of the village and swam slowly in counterclockwise circles. Every ten stokes or so, he dove under, and upon surfacing, he floated motionless, as if dead. After quietly leaving the river, he scrubbed his body with nettles, plants with burrs on their leaves that stung and reddened the skin.

Next, he dressed in a bearskin robe and a headband of cedar bark. After painting certain marks on his face, he entered a small house that had a ridgepole and brace poles but no planks, so it was open and people could see him. The house contained the remains of previous leaders, and as the chief sang to them and prayed, he asked that his people share their power. Whenever Maquina entered the house, he was accompanied by Ya-tintla-no. She tied a rope around his waist and held on to the other end. As the chief pulled her in circles, he said, "This is how mah-hack will act." It was one of many scenes that Jewitt witnessed that made no sense, at least at first.

The Nootka repeated this ceremony in December at the waxing of the moon, twice at Cooptee and four times at Friendly Cove, where Maquina swam in the ocean and dragged his body over reefs covered with barnacles. His paddlers scrubbed themselves with nettles during these ceremonies and kept toughening themselves until the waxing of the moon in April. At the chief's signal, four canoes were launched in a rush, and the entire village, except for Ya-tintla-no, was drumming. She was lying motionless in the chief's bed, as if about to die.

Soon, Maquina's boat was on the trail of a forty-ton gray whale that measured fifty feet in length. The fact that the Nootka hunted whale—and had been hunting whale for two thousand years without the use of metal products—hit Jewitt like no other thing he witnessed while a captive. He could not believe that they dared to do it. He could not understand how they hoped to succeed. He wondered what the first hunt was like thousands of years ago and how many

Nootka had been killed over the years when the whales passed by in their annual migration. What he learned about whaling, he recorded with unchecked passion. Jewitt had finally found adventure and the wonders of the unknown.

The hunt began miles from the village and often in rough seas. As the lead canoe gained on the whale, the other boats stayed in a line behind so the animal couldn't see them when it surfaced for air. When the lead boat neared the animal's tail, the chief readied his harpoon, a ten-foot shaft of yew wood tipped with barbs made from antler. Because the harpoon wasn't thrown but was thrust into the whale, it was necessary to get within a few feet. And the whale had to be struck while diving or else the chief's boat would be smashed by its thrashing. At just the right moment, when he was close enough and the whale was about to dive, Maquina's canoe sprinted from the back and moved up to the left side. Leaning over the bow as far as he dared, Maquina struck the whale at a spot just behind one of its flippers.

The next two minutes was the most dangerous time for the hunters. After striking the whale, the chief dropped beneath the bow, paddlers swung the canoe to the left, and six hundred feet of cedar rope started zinging out of the boat. The paddlers on the left watched for tangles in the coils of rope in the bottom of the boat. The paddlers on the right ducked to avoid being knocked overboard by the rope. Bouncing and rolling in the wake of the whale, the canoe was hit with sheets of water until the boat was behind the whale, which was towing it across the ocean. When the harpoon's shaft broke free, the fastest boat rushed it to the village. A subchief held the shaft over the chief's wife, who started thrashing and crying to hasten the whale's death.

Usually, a single harpoon didn't kill a whale, but the animal felt the sting and sometimes turned and charged, swamping boats and drowning entire crews. To slow the whale and make its diving more difficult, the men attached air-filled seal and sea lion bladders to the rope to act as floats. When the whale slowed, the hunters stuck it with a second and then a third harpoon, each fixed with a rope and floats. Some whales could tow four boats and fifty floats for four days before they weakened and surfaced.

When the whale could pull no more, the chief thrust a spear into its heart, and six men dove overboard and swam as fast as they could to the whale's head. They had eight minutes to tie the whale's mouth shut, or else it would take in water and sink—and the entire effort would be lost. In those frantic moments, they used daggers to punch holes in the whale's lips and then tie its mouth shut with rope, as it thrashed and rolled until it was finally still. Floats were tied to its body to keep it on the surface while it was towed to shore. If the tide was right and there were no sharks, the boats might cover fifty miles in two days to reach the village.

Only chiefs could take whale, and the difficulty of succeeding at this was evident in the first week of hunting at Friendly Cove. Maquina stuck three whales, but each time the tip of his harpoon broke off. Because the prongs would break or be pulled out while the canoes were being towed, many chiefs took no more than three whales in their entire lifetimes, and some took none. Having failed in the previous season, Maquina was short-tempered and unhappy, until Jewitt stepped forward with a grand idea. He was so caught up in the excitement that he suggested making a harpoon tip for the chief—forged of steel. On the very next day, Maquina's shaft arrived and was held over his wife's thrashing body. The village began drumming to thank Quahootze and to pray that the harpoon would hold fast.

Three days later, the canoes appeared in Friendly Cove towing Maquina's whale. The paddlers sang towing songs and praised the whale, telling it to prepare for a royal welcome. The people on the housetops were drumming and cheering, and from the bow of his boat, Maquina was shouting, "Kah-ah-coh mah-hack! Kah-ah-coh mah-hack" ("I bring the whale")! He had not lost the power of those who had come before him, and his wife had acted just right. Every tribe along the coast already knew of his conquest. But they did not know about his harpoon.

The whale was beached at high tide and butchered on shore. Using shells with razor-sharp edges, workers sliced a two-foot section of blubber from the head to the dorsal fin. The twenty-foot slab of meat was called the "chief's cut" and was considered sacred. Ya-tintla-no and Maquina's other wives carried the cut to the chief's house, where it was decorated with feathers and displayed in his quarters. For the next four days, it was honored with singing, fasting, and praying. Maquina told the guest, "We are glad you have come to visit us. We have been saving these feathers for you for a long time."

Others said, "What a great whale you are!" and, "How fat you are!"

Like spoiled salmon, whale blubber was considered a great delicacy and was eaten at a superfeast. Only guests were allowed to eat the chief's cut, but before eating they had to watch the prince dance for two hours and then listen to Maquina's speech, all the while trying not to appear too anxious. There was food for all, Maquina said, and much oil to be enjoyed, until all stomachs were full and everyone was happy. Since a gray whale produced about ten thousand quarts of train oil, there was indeed much oil, and much would be left over. Jewitt was offered a portion of blubber, which he described as "tasteless but not intolerable." Of Nootka whaling, he wrote, "I have not seen or heard of such bravery. They are a courageous people and capable of great things." It was a big leap for him, and he almost forgot whom he was talking about.

Jewitt's excitement about whaling was cut short by a string of bad events, all of which were blamed on the captives. First, Tootoosch died, and his death was attributed to the ghosts of Hall and Wood, who no doubt had been summoned by the captives. Next, Jewitt and Thompson were thought to be responsible for the scarcity of salmon in Friendly Cove. It was believed that they had called upon their dead shipmates in the cove to chase the salmon out. And third, Maquina's rivals learned about his superharpoon and made plans to attack the chief and kill Jewitt, or else take Jewitt captive so they could have a superharpoon. Jewitt's great idea had backfired. Instead of helping him stay alive, it threatened his life.

In describing how he and Thompson were tormented, Jewitt's writing was concise, as if he had been trying to cram in as much as possible before he died. The Nootka called the captives "wretched slaves" and made them douse the latrines with powder. They asked what had happened to their tyee, Captain Salter, and the Nootka gestured that he was dead. Maquina couldn't stop his people from treating the captives poorly because he was in the minority, and the prince and his mother were of no help because they were nowhere to be found. The Natives even went out of their way to offend Thompson, which wasn't hard to do. With all that was on his mind, Jewitt had to restrain the sailmaker from charging and fighting back.

It isn't possible to know what Maquina was thinking at this time, but a good guess might be that he was thinking, *If anyone believes they can do a better job, then they're welcome to try.* His main concern was being attacked by his enemies, and not just because they wanted a steel-tipped harpoon. Several villages to the north had turned against him because ships no longer stopped to trade after the massacre of the *Boston* crew, and these villages planned to avenge the loss of trade. And some of Maquina's subchiefs were plotting against him; they planned to overthrow him for his having made the mistake of dumping the bodies from the *Boston* into Friendly Cove, where they were haunting the salmon.

Maquina's plan to keep himself and Jewitt alive was to arm his captives and make them his personal bodyguards. Jewitt and Thompson were given muskets and ordered to stay with the chief around the clock. They fired the *Boston*'s cannon at one and four in the morning to discourage an attack at night, and they frisked subchiefs before they counseled with Maquina. This crazy turnabout, Jewitt said, "led [him and Thompson] to the point of utter hopelessness and despair." Here he was right. If he lost Maquina, then it was over for him and Thompson as well.

The event that solved the latest crisis occurred at the pond. Jewitt and Thompson were washing clothes when they encountered Nootka from another village. As Maquina's people had, these visitors insulted the two men, in spite of Thompson's mean look. One was bolder than the others and walked on a blanket that Thompson had spread on the grass to dry. Thompson dared the man to do it again, and when he did, Thompson overtook him and cut off his head. It was hard for Jewitt to see, and he didn't spend much time describing it.

The others who were at the pond fled and spread word of Thompson's power. Thompson carried the man's head back to the village, and when he and Jewitt entered, the Nootka were so frightened that they ran into their houses. Not Maquina, however, who was pleased at the sight. Thompson's decapitating of the Nootka man led Maquina's enemies to cancel their war plans. In addition, the subchiefs backed off, and so the harassment of the captives eased up. Thompson had finally connected with the Nootka, and Jewitt was happy to write, "This had a favorable effect for us, not only with the other tribes, but with the local inhabitants, who treated us afterwards with less disrespect." As to Thompson's act of savagery, Jewitt was silent.

Seven

LE YAR EE YEE YAH!

The harpoon Jewitt had fashioned for Maquina elevated the chief in status above all other chiefs. There was another speech and more dancing before rivals ate his second whale. A week later, they were called for a third, and then for a fourth, which was given special status. By the time the fourth whale arrived, there was a backlog of blubber, so Maquina allowed the whale to rot on the beach. When paddling toward the village, the guests could smell the delicacy from miles away. Once they arrived, they had to listen to a long speech and watch another dance, before they could eat the putrid blubber in a feast to end all feasts. His powerful display made it clear that Maquina didn't need to take a fifth whale, because everyone knew that he could if he wanted to.

Around the time the second whale arrived, Jewitt began to see that his great idea might not have been so great after all. And by the time the fourth whale arrived, he was a wreck, and his head hurt as bad as ever. Killing four whales in one season was unheard of, and now every chief at every feast demanded a steel-tipped harpoon. When Jewitt said, "Week-eatish" ("I have no more"), they came back stronger, saying, "Sick-a-minny eenapukseem mah-hack" ("Iron harpoon for whale")! Now he dreaded whaling and wished that Maquina would stop it.

Maquina's whales put Jewitt's life in danger again, but this time he had only himself to blame. The chief told him that if he made harpoon tips for others, he would have him killed. If he tried to join another group, he would have him killed. And if he refused to join another group, he would be marked for death by Maquina's rivals, who couldn't tolerate a permanent loss of their status. Once again, they were planning to attack Maquina and kill or kidnap Jewitt. The chief told Jewitt to stay armed and make more tips, in case he wasn't around in the future.

On the other hand, Maquina was in a tough position, too. His job was to elevate his people above others, which he had done, and to share his good fortune with others, which he had done. In doing so, he put his life on the line, and the easy way out would have been to kill the captive. But Maquina would never do that just to save his own life. He liked Jewitt and treated him as a friend, taking him hunting at Tashees and fishing at Cooptee. There was only one reason why Maquina would kill him: for the benefit of the group—that is, if he tried to defect, if he was about to be kidnapped, or if the whites came for revenge.

While describing the latest threat to his life, Jewitt wrote about Nootka humor. More than likely, he had become so accustomed to impending death that it wasn't a special event anymore. Switching subjects was also good therapy. Suddenly, he was laughing with the Nootka and writing about Maquina's climmer-habbee.

All chiefs had a climmer-habbee, who was a sort of master of ceremonies, news reporter, and court jester. Maquina's was named Kinclemet, and he was valued for his ability to make people laugh. He mimicked various situations, such as a hunter's being chased by a wolf and leaving a trail of feathers for the wolf to follow. The Nootka used dentalium shells for money, and Kinclemet made the shells disappear and then reappear in greater quantity. At the feast of the putrid whale, he ate four salmon and swallowed nearly a gallon of train oil. Guests watched in anticipation and laughed wildly as the joker vomited into two bowls. A year ago, Jewitt would have considered such behavior vulgar. Now it made him laugh, which was better for his mental health than always stressing the negative.

Usually, Kinclemet acted out stories that he had concocted, and most involved the chief. On one occasion, he wore Maquina's whaling bonnet and played the chief on a hunt. He was attacked by sharks and broke several weapons in fighting them off. An octopus jumped on his face and knocked him overboard, and when he emerged from the water, his face was covered with orange dots.

After enacting more mishaps, Kinclemet disappeared behind some boxes and reappeared dressed in a robe made from whale blubber. He swam in circles, hopped a bit, and then set the robe on fire, saying, "Een-nuk-see mah-hack!" ("Fire whale!"), along with other words used to indicate that the whale was preparing itself to be eaten. After the fire was doused, he ripped the robe to pieces and hurled the smoldering meat into the crowd. Jewitt described the airborne blubber as "hilarious to the point that I could not speak from laughing." That was fine, but he missed the real meaning of the stunt. The Nootka poked fun at their leaders to reinforce the idea that the group was more important than any one person. Poking fun at Maquina was part of what made Kinclemet so popular.

Starting in early June, Jewitt's writing shifted to war, and his attitude toward the subject was nonchalant at first, as if it was just the next thing to happen and he should record it. In preparing themselves, the warriors bathed in Friendly Cove six times a day over the course of a month. They scrubbed their bodies with briars until their skin bled. They numbered around a hundred, and as they toughened themselves, they shouted, "Wocash, Quahootze!" and spoke other phrases to express, "Great God! Let me live, not be sick, find the enemy, and not fear him." They stayed apart from their wives for a month and fasted during this time period. Some would be killed in the upcoming war, and their wives would marry other men who would care for them even though already married themselves.

Maquina told Jewitt, who was already making daggers, to create a spiked club that could kill with one blow. Jewitt accepted the challenge with enthusiasm. Once finished, the weapon measured a foot and a half in length and was made entirely of steel. The handle had a crook, or turn, so it couldn't be easily wrenched from someone's hand, and the six-inch-long spike at the other end was welded to a steel knob. Using his own imagination, Jewitt fashioned the back of the knob to resemble a man's face with an open mouth, as if screaming. Polished to a bright shine, the weapon exceeded Maquina's expectations, and Jewitt was proud of the work.

He learned that the chief was preparing to attack a village some fifty miles to the south. There were two reasons for the expedition: to discourage rivals from attacking Maquina and to square an offense, the details of which weren't shared with the captive. Nor did the chief say why the captives would be going along, only that they would. Doubtless it was to keep them alive, because if left behind, they might be killed by rivals or subchiefs. That was less important to Jewitt than the fact that he was going to war.

Twenty canoes left at midnight amid drumming and people's singing, "Le yar ee yee yah" ("Poorly can our foes contend with us when we come with our daggers")! The Nootka came only with daggers, as was the custom, but Jewitt and Thompson were given pistols, meaning that they weren't expected to be neutral observers in the war. Jewitt's expression didn't match the one on the face he had carved into Maquina's weapon—not yet, anyway—but he was afraid. He never mentioned Thompson's state of mind, but it would be reasonable to conclude that Thompson was ready to rumble.

The party reached the enemy's village about two hours before sunrise, and the chief ordered that they rest and then attack an hour before sunrise, at the time of deepest sleep. It was the Nootka way of war, which was understood by all: dispatch the enemy while they slept. These rules of engagement, however, didn't apply when they attacked whites. The village of five hundred residents was situated atop a steep hill. The warriors climbed up in near silence and entered the village from behind.

Of all aspects of Nootka culture, Jewitt judged their way of war most harshly. He said it was "cruel," "barbarous," and "inhumane"—which it was, like all warfare. But was it cruel because the Nootka used knives instead of guns? Was it barbarous because they used a sneak attack and killed for revenge? Did it matter how many they killed—ten, a hundred, eleven million? How could they be judged inhumane when people killing other people was as old as humanity itself? All killing is barbarous and horrible. Jewitt judged it harshly because the killing he saw seemed unique, like the *Boston*.

The operation started when Maquina entered the chief's house, crawling on his hands and knees, and when warriors entered the other houses in like fashion. The captives were told to guard the entrance to the great house and stop anyone from entering to make a rescue. Jewitt didn't want to stain his hands with the blood of a fellow human being, and for that he is to be admired. Thompson was just the opposite, however. He considered the Nootka to be so inferior that he would only use a knife against them. As Maquina took out the chief with his club, he let out a fierce war-whoop, and the fight was on. Jewitt could hear the screaming inside and envisioned Maquina's weapon in action. Now his face was like the face on the club, and he regretted having made it.

The contest lasted about twenty minutes, until the enemy saw that further resistance was futile and surrendered. Some escaped, more were killed, and the survivors were taken as slaves. Jewitt never said how many his side lost, but he did note that he had taken four prisoners—somehow, and without shedding blood. Thompson was challenged by seven warriors and he killed them all, connecting with the Nootka once again. Maquina was so impressed that he designated Thompson a chehiel-suma-har—a mythical warrior whose feats were recalled when preparing for war. The men carried booty to the canoes and enjoyed an uneventful trip back to the village. Maquina appeared much like he had on the deck of the *Boston,* casual and relaxed.

Except for the people who were defeated, everyone benefited from the war. Thompson was revered, Maquina's rivals canceled their plans to attack, and no one wanted Jewitt dead—at least for the moment. Switching tactics, the other groups tried to buy Jewitt, and although the chief was polite in hearing them out, he said no. Delegation after delegation sat through the chief's speeches about the victory and endured the prince's dancing before accepting loot from the war, along with more blubber. Also included in each potlatch was Maquina's account of his chehiel-suma-har's exploits, both at the pond and in war. Not surprisingly, no one tried to buy Thompson.

The offers to buy Jewitt provided him with an opportunity for escape, and he took it. During the summer, he wrote sixteen letters and gave them to different chiefs, hoping that one letter might reach a trading ship. Because they wanted to win him over, the chiefs accepted the letters, and a few even accepted Jewitt's argument that if he defected, Maquina would kill them, so the better way was to aid in his return to the white world. It was good logic and showed Jewitt's understanding of Nootka thinking: the next best thing to having Jewitt was denying him to Maquina.

Chief Utilla was most persistent in trying to buy the captive, and when Jewitt slipped him a letter, Utilla promised to give it to the first ship he spotted. In gratitude, Jewitt made a war club similar to Maquina's and gave it to the chief when no one was looking. He had planned to make a harpoon for Utilla, but before he could start the work, the village began moving to Tashees. Thinking that he had put one over on Maquina, Jewitt wrote that the chief trusted him and "believed my pledges of loyalty to his people." Not really, as he would soon discover.

A new chapter in his life began shortly after Tashees was constructed. Aware of Jewitt's duplicity, Maquina told him that he had to become Nootka or die. After a year and a half, it was clear that the whites weren't coming, so it was also clear that the captive would be around for some time. By making him Nootka, he would be loyal to the group, and rivals would stop trying to buy him. He had no choice but to go along. The only question was how much of a Nootka he would have to be.

For starters, Maquina told him that the four men he had taken in battle were his slaves. They would do his laundry and any other work he ordered them to do, which was fine with Jewitt and also fine with Thompson, who would share "his son's" slaves, since he didn't have any of his own. Next, Jewitt would be more content, Maquina said, if he took a wife, so he was ordered to find one. "Reduced to this sad state," Jewitt wrote at Tashees, "with death on one side and matrimony on the other, I thought it proper to choose the lesser of the two evils and consented to be married." His writing was like this sometimes, using the word *evil* loosely.

Since there were no women in the village whom Jewitt found suitable, workers loaded canoes with gifts, and a delegation left to find a wife for Jewitt. The party of fifty men proceeded to the village of Chief Upquesta. After a feast, Kinclemet made a spectacular entrance, whistling, rattling, running in circles, and all the while shouting, "Tooteyoohannis! Tooteyoohannis!" which was the name the Nootka had given to Jewitt. Kinclemet yelled that Tooteyoohannis was "chee-so-check-up" ("a good man") and different from them only in that he was white. He said that this white man was a valuable person who could make daggers and harpoons. He was loved by all for his great qualities. Sat-sat-sok-sis loved Tooteyoohannis. Kinclemet gave the impression that it was a hard sell, which it was. Being white among the Nootka wasn't a trivial matter.

When Kinclemet finished, Upquesta gave the okay for Jewitt to make a selection. It wasn't clear what he was looking for, but on his third pass through the house he stopped at Upquesta's table, where a seventeen-year-old girl caught his eye. The chief signaled for her to stand, and his climmer-habbee announced that she was the princess Yuqua, the chief's only daughter. The climmer-habbee started rattling and humming, and others joined in.

As gifts were carried into the house, the drumming on the roof became louder, as did the rattling and humming. Whenever an article was placed before Upquesta, Kinclemet shouted its virtues: "Cham-mas-shis so-har!" ("Sweet salmon!") and "Ly ah-ish klack-e-miss" ("Much oil")! With each proclamation, Upquesta flashed a look of disapproval, but near the end of the giving, he assumed a neutral look and his people began chanting, "Klack-ko-Tyee" ("Thank you, Chief")!

Afterward, Maquina delivered a speech detailing Jewitt's great qualities, and Upquesta followed with a speech of the same length, saying that he loved Yuqua and couldn't bear to part with his only daughter. Following the give-and-take, Upquesta hinted that he would approve the marriage, and this made Kinclemet explode with excitement. Jewitt wrote that the jester "cut a thousand capers, spinning on his heels like a top and screaming at the top of his lungs, 'Wocash, Tyee! Wocash, Tyee!'"

According to the custom, Upquesta returned the gifts to Jewitt and added a gift of two slaves, which Jewitt knew to accept to show respect. Jewitt's slaves loaded his possessions into a canoe, and Yuqua boarded, smiling. She liked him from the moment he entered the house and was glad to be attached to a such famous person, even if his people were bad.

In spite of the title of his book, *The Adventures and Sufferings of John R. Jewitt,* Jewitt enjoyed a fine captivity at Tashees. No one was trying to kill him. He had a wife, six slaves, and wealth. The future looked good, and he could play Tooteyoohannis because he had seen all there was to see with the Nootka, he thought.

Eight

TOOTEYOOHANNIS

Yuqua's reception at Tashees exceeded any celebration that Jewitt had seen, and he played Tooteyoohannis amid "terrible deafening noise." Blunderbusses and pistols were fired. Cloth and silk was hurled in the air. As soon as Maquina landed, he joined others on the roof of the great house, and Thompson fired the cannon three times, making the people even more excited. The village understood the meaning of the marriage: Tooteyoohannis was now one of them, and any attack on him would be revenged by Maquina, Upquesta, and their allies. After Yuqua was taken away, Jewitt stepped ashore and was surrounded by women who stroked his arms and said, "Ly ah-ish tanassis check-up" ("Many sons"). He acted as if he knew that Yuqua would be taken away, showing disinterest and telling his slaves to unload his possessions.

After ten days of isolation, Yuqua was led into the great house and was seated at Maquina's table. Jewitt greeted her casually to show that he knew it was time for her to return. Secretly, he expected an elaborate wedding, including a dance by the prince and a speech by Kinclemet. None of it happened. After a feast, the two were considered married, without exchanging vows or receiving congratulations, which had already been given upon the princess's arrival at the village. She had been kept pure for ten days and had received instructions regarding her duties to ensure that the marriage lasted.

Tooteyoohannis had no complaints about his wife. He said that she was "friendly, intelligent, and the handsomest of their women with the exception of Maquina's queen." He said that she had long, black hair, a "youthful sensuality," and a desire to please. Every time he spoke to her, she said, "Woho, woho" ("Very well, very well"), obedient to his every wish. She bathed twice a day to keep her skin smooth. She changed jewelry and decorated her robe with ribbons. On certain days, she left down on Jewitt's pillow and even made inquiries about his people, asking how strong they were and if the women were pleasing to the men.

Jewitt played the role of husband to some extent. He exchanged oil for bracelets and necklaces, which Yuqua accepted with delight. He told his slaves what food she liked and let her take what she wanted from his possessions—needles, silk, and rabbit fur. But he wouldn't wear the kutsacks she made, and he didn't need her help when he was working. While Yuqua had put aside concerns that her husband was from a savage land, he wrote, "A compulsory marriage with the most beautiful person in the world can never prove a source of happiness, and I could not help but view my wife as a chain that was to bind me to this savage land." While she sought the advice of other women to help her be a better wife, he schemed to use his marriage as a bargaining chip.

Jewitt told Maquina that he would be a better husband if he were permitted to wear the white man's clothes. The chief allowed it, but he forbade Jewitt to cut his hair or use the English language. Then Jewitt said that he might love Yuqua more if he were to be excused from attending ceremonies. The chief said no but told him that he could limit his participation to rattling and drumming. He could go to the pond on Sunday and decline to go to war, but he couldn't decline Yuqua's advances when she said, "Tooteyoohannis, come to my desire," or words to that effect. Her best chance at bringing him around was to bear his son, and Maquina made his concessions with the same goal in mind.

Now that he was Nootka, Jewitt witnessed events that were new to him. He wrote about these, having by now dropped Yuqua as a subject, evidently deciding that he had adequately covered the topic. At one gathering in November, Kinclemet spoke for four hours. In bursts of fifteen minutes or so, he related some experience and then ran out of the house while the audience drummed, as if applauding. Each time Kinclemet reappeared, he wore a different mask: a wolf, a deer, and so on. The drumming stopped when he started speaking, often with his head turned upward, as though talking to an empty building. Occasionally, he faced the audience and screamed, as though telling them off.

Kinclemet said that a young chief and an old man went porpoise hunting and found themselves surrounded by a school of killer whales, *drumming, rattling, stop.* As the whales surfaced, they made a loud noise, and the old man said, "I am beginning to feel faint. These must be supernatural killer whales," *drumming, rattling,* and so on. They followed the whales to an island, and the old man could see that the whales were headed for the beach. "They are going to become something else now," he said. "Wait until they do, and you will 'get' whatever it is." The whales surfaced, howled four times like wolves, then became wolves and ran into the forest, leaving in the mind of the young chief the supernatural songs of the wolf, *drumming, rattling.*

In another story, he described a house in the mountains where everything that passed by it died. Even birds that flew over the house died, and their skeletons covered the ground. When a young chief approached, the house turned into a boulder, and the women in front of the house turned into foam, which the chief sopped up with his robe to learn their songs.

Jewitt couldn't understand the point of every story, but most were about acquiring power from supernatural forces, like acquiring strength through prayer. Yuqua had heard some of the stories, and she rattled and drummed with her husband.

Other than occasionally noting her presence, Jewitt continued to focus on other events. He mentioned one of Maquina's speeches in which the chief related the great accomplishments of his ancestors, but Maquina didn't mention his four whales because it would have been in bad taste. The villagers held funerals where they cremated the bodies along with salmon and silk from the *Boston*. A climmer-habbee from another village announced that a boat and its crew were lost, either in a storm or because white devils had attacked. Sat-sat-sok-sis was honored for taking a deer at Friendly Cove. Jewitt's journal reads like the news of the day—news from another world, however, not from his own. He was sailing along, happily playing Tooteyoohannis, until December 13 hit and the tribute to Quahootze began. He hadn't experienced it the year before when he was banished to a hut, but now he was allowed to see the critical ceremony.

The start of the ceremony caught Jewitt by surprise, as it would any outsider. On the morning of December 13, Maquina fired a musket from his quarters, and Sat-sat-sok-sis fell to the ground as if dead. The women in the house screamed that the prince was dead and began tearing handfuls of hair from their heads. Hearing drumming on the roof, warriors ran into the house and inquired about the cause of the trauma. They were followed by two men wearing wolf skins and the heads of wolves, and they entered the house on their hands and knees and carried the prince off on their backs. Jewitt watched without a clue of what it meant. He later learned that it was a prelude to worship.

Once the prince was gone, the village assembled in Maquina's house, except for the drummers, who remained on the roof. Regardless of rank, all wore plain dress with no ornaments, and their heads were bound with fillet—a strip of fish meat worn like a headband. Showing dejection and often crying, they sang about salmon and other animals, and also of their longing for God. Maquina kept time by beating on a drum while others rattled. They sang and wept until it was dark and they left, returning at midnight to start again. Jewitt kept rattling with Yuqua by his side, noting that she was in a trance and gave little indication of being his wife. After the first week, the headbands started to rot, and Jewitt complained in his journal that everyone "smelled horribly." The other participants would disagree.

Other than smelling the odor of the headbands and being hungry from fasting, Jewitt was doing fine until the last day of the ceremony. At the start of the day, at midnight, men began poking their arms with knives, and women began gouging their scalps with shells. In time, Maquina and his family had been cut, and Yuqua's hair was bloody. Warriors who had made themselves bloody ran through the house screaming, "Klooskosh Quahootze!" ("Great Quahootze!"), and when they approached Maquina's table, Jewitt averted his eyes. "I could not see such bloodshed," he said, "and I could not gaze upon my wife's bloody hands." He wrote that the Nootka were "depraved for inflicting pain on themselves," although they saw the act as a demonstration of their faith in God. Most religions, at one time in their histories, practiced bloodletting. Meanwhile, Natives in the New World were being killed in the name of Jewitt's God.

The theme of sickness dominated Jewitt's writing at Cooptee, and his entries were brief. Before leaving Tashees, he had lost Captain Salter's coat, and by January, still in Cooptee, the last of his clothing had worn out. His only protection was a piece of cloth about two yards long, and he had a cold that was so bad that he couldn't work or go to the woods on Sunday. Now he wore one of Yuqua's kutsacks, but it was too late to be of much help. In addition, Thompson couldn't walk because he had rheumatism in one of his knees. He wasn't getting better, either. Fortunately, because he was Tooteyoohannis, Jewitt had food and a wife to care for him. He needed her now.

The downward slide continued after the tribe returned to Friendly Cove. By March 1805, at the two-year mark of his captivity, Jewitt had pneumonia. He couldn't rise from bed, he could keep down only water, and his chest hurt so bad that he expected to die. There were no ships to rescue him, Thompson still couldn't walk, and Yuqua's potions of roots and herbs only made him vomit. His fear was that if he died, he would not have a Christian burial. Yuqua pleaded for him to fight, saying, "Cha-alt-see klat-tur wah" ("Go off" or "Go away"). She was speaking to his illness, demanding that it leave his body.

Jewitt's illness finally did leave, and when he could stand, Maquina put him to work making harpoon tips. The chief was obsessed with having an adequate supply, and he grumbled when the captive quit work after a few hours each day. Following a relapse that lasted a week, Jewitt used his work to bargain with the chief.

He said that he could work better if he could part with his wife, whom he still saw as binding him to a "savage land." It was an easy call, because Yuqua hadn't produced a son or any child, and she was less important than harpoon tips, which were beneficial to the entire village. When Jewitt told Yuqua that their marriage was over, she begged to stay, saying that no one could take better care of Tooteyoohannis. When she was forced to return to her village, she departed in tears, leaving her gifts behind. "I would miss her expressions of love and mildness of manners," Jewitt wrote, as if she had drifted off into space somewhere and he had nothing to do with it.

During the summer of 1805, Jewitt's journal entries rambled from one subject to the next. He mentioned that a shaman had cured Thompson's rheumatism, and right afterward he mentioned Tootoosch's death, which he had already covered. He made a brief reference to a woman praying in the woods, and he followed this with a discussion of the depth of the water at Friendly Cove. He wrote about whether or not he had correctly counted the days of his captivity, and then he provided a description of the traps set for bear, which he had covered already. The journal entry ended with his comment that the Nootka were "a remarkably modest people." This statement makes no sense in the context of the other events he discussed, and it also contradicts his observation that the Nootka were a "half-naked" people.

Besides suffering from depression, it was clear that something was seriously wrong with Jewitt. He still had a fever, and the wound to his head was still aching. He may have been losing his mind, for, like Tootoosch, he refused to eat. In writing about his third summer at Friendly Cove, he said nothing about whaling, the subject that had excited him the most, and made no mention of the prince, the prince's mother, food gathering, or ceremonies. Instead, he wrote that if he died, he would like to be buried near the shore of the pond. Thompson could dig the grave and give him a Christian burial, and also hide the journal so it could later be recovered for the world to read.

Nine

THE LYDIA

J
ewitt's fever was gone by July, and his head didn't hurt so bad. He could hold down food and work a normal day making daggers. Maquina was preparing for war again, and as his men scrubbed with briars, Thompson and the prince helped at Jewitt's forge. The chehiel-suma-har announced that he wouldn't be going to war because he needed to stay with his son. Now Thompson was acting as though he really was Jewitt's father, with real feelings toward him. After his recovery, Jewitt mentioned that he saw Yuqua when her people came for a potlatch. She rattled and whistled, but the two never talked—and there was no mention of recovering her gifts.

Jewitt's main hope was that he be rescued before the village moved to Tashees, which would occur in about six weeks. On July 15, he wrote that there were seven ships along the coast, according to Kinclemet, and that their captains still feared Friendly Cove. In the sixteen letters he had previously written and given to chiefs, Jewitt had pleaded for a rescue. Now he wrote about the contents of those letters.

His letters explained Maquina's reasons for taking the *Boston*. His people had been robbed and killed by whites and were dying from diseases spread by sailors. If a ship would enter Friendly Cove and extend courtesy and respect, Maquina would reciprocate, so there was no reason to be afraid. Jewitt had reached an all-time high in understanding the Nootka and telling the truth. Thompson still didn't care about the Natives, but he had clearly mellowed. On the morning of July 19, the two were working at the forge when they heard the boom of a cannon amid Natives' shouting, "Mamethlee! Mamethlee" ("White men! White men")!

There was a trading ship anchored in Friendly Cove, but Jewitt didn't know if the captain had one of his letters. Maybe. His heart was pounding. *This was it—after two and a half years—and it might be the only chance for escape.* He didn't look up. He kept hammering metal while his mind raced to devise a plan. He told Thompson not to speak but to act as if nothing was happening, deciding that it was best to do nothing until he knew more. A party of warriors ran by them and into the great house. Jewitt and Thompson kept working without looking up.

As events unfolded, it was clear that a bond between Maquina and his captive had been built over the years. Jewitt was aware of it and somehow knew that the chief would hesitate to kill him if a ship came along—and this delay would allow him time to carry out a plan. It started when the chief asked him if he had heard about the ship, and he said that it meant nothing to him. Still probing, Maquina asked, "Tooteyoohannis, you no glad go board?" and Jewitt answered that he had no wish to leave the village. Two years ago, Maquina would have killed Jewitt at the sight of a trading ship. Now he hesitated, but the chief wasn't sure if he should board the ship. It was anchored three miles off shore and was just sitting there, as if the captain wasn't sure of his next move, either.

When asked to attend the council meeting to discuss what to do, Jewitt came as Tooteyoohannis, thoroughly Nootka, by design. He had painted his body black and had painted red squares on his face. He had tied his long hair at the top of his head, and he was wearing a bearskin robe. As he sat waiting to be called upon, the council considered three options: kill the crew, pretend that a different tribe had taken the *Boston*, or hide the captives in the woods. When the council couldn't agree, the discussion turned to whether Maquina should board the ship to determine the captain's intentions. "Wik! Wik!" ("No! No!"), everyone shouted, believing that those on the ship would kill the chief to avenge the crew of the *Boston*. Maquina said that he wasn't afraid of boarding and would be guided by Tooteyoohannis, who had been saying all along that whites weren't into revenge.

When called upon, Jewitt spoke in the best Nootka he could muster. He was animated, like a climmer-habbee. For the thousandth time, he explained the trading practices of whites and emphasized that the sailors weren't warriors. Besides, they were too weak to overpower the Nootka, who were so brave that they could defeat any enemy. The ship had come for trade or resupplying, he said, and in either case the village would benefit. He didn't know this to be true, but he considered it the best thing to say if he had any chance of rescue.

Because they believed that the whites had to avenge the massacre of the *Boston*, not a single Nootka bought Jewitt's argument. But the speech may have served Maquina's purpose, which was to trade with the ship, if possible. He said that he would board the ship if Tooteyoohannis wrote a letter saying that the captives had been treated well and that Maquina was a good man. Jewitt said that he would write the letter and say those things because they were true. Instead, he wrote the following:

To Captain ————————,
of the Brig. ————————.
Nootka, July 19, 1805.

Sir,

The bearer of this letter is the Indian king by the name of Maquina. He was the instigator of the capture of the ship *Boston*, of Boston, in North America, John Salter, captain, and of the murder of twenty-five men of her crew, the only two survivors being now on shore——. Wherefore I hope you will take care to confine him and watch him so he cannot escape. By so doing, we shall be able to obtain our release in the course of a few hours.

John R. Jewitt, Armorer of the *Boston*,
for himself, and
John Thompson, Sailmaker of the said ship.

Maquina's eyes could look right through a person. When Jewitt gave him the letter, he handed it back and asked for an explanation of each line. Jewitt pointed to the first line and said that it mentioned how kindly the Nootka had treated him and Thompson. The next line, he said, told the captain to give rum to Maquina, and the last lines urged the captain to trade with the chief, who practiced fair exchange.

Maquina looked into Jewitt's eyes for the truth. He might have been thinking that Jewitt had stopped writing in his journal, had gone hunting and fishing with the chief, was a friend to the prince and his mother, and so on. Placing his finger on Jewitt's signature, he looked at him with intensity and asked, "John, you no lie?"

He answered, "Why do you ask me such a question, Tyee? Have you ever known me to lie?"

"No," Maquina said.

Jewitt responded, "Then how can you suppose that I should tell you a lie now?" The chief kept staring at him and then broke off, saying that he believed him. It was the sixth lie Jewitt told Maquina and one of his best.

As Maquina prepared to leave for the ship, his people became frantic. Subchiefs argued against his going, and women pulled on their hair and cried. The chief's wives begged him not to trust the white man, but he pushed them aside and kept saying, "John no lie." He left with ten prime skins as a gift, and at a short distance from shore, he gave his captive a final test. He called to Jewitt, asking if he wanted to board the ship. Anticipating such a move, Jewitt shouted back, "Tooteyoohannis, Nootka! Tooteyoohannis, Nootka!" Jewitt hadn't involved Thompson in the scheme so he couldn't botch it up.

After some time, Maquina's canoe returned without the chief. The entire village was on the beach, and as the canoe neared, the people could hear the paddlers screaming that Jewitt had said bad things in his letter and that Maquina had been taken prisoner. It was true. Upon boarding, the chief presented the letter to Captain Samuel Hill of the *Lydia,* who was already in receipt of the letter Jewitt had given to Chief Utilla. Acting calmly, Hill read Maquina's letter and offered him rum, and when the chief relaxed, crew members overpowered him and took him below deck.

The loss of Maquina caused mass confusion and led the Nootka to shout, "Klooskosh Quahootze! I-yee ma hak" ("Great God! I do not understand")! Women knelt before Jewitt and begged him to save the chief. The prince began crying, and other children followed his lead. Jewitt had figured correctly. Maquina was the village, and his people would do anything to save their tyee. There were few kings, queens, or presidents anywhere in the world who could claim to be loved more by their people.

Jewitt guessed what was coming next and so he appeared calm and relaxed, as Maquina did when he was certain of himself. When warriors told Jewitt that they would cut him into pieces no bigger than their thumbnails, he looked away as though he couldn't hear them. When they said they would hang him by his heels and burn him over a fire, he acted bored. Eventually, the subchiefs intervened and asked Jewitt if the captain intended to kill Maquina, which was the question he had been waiting for. "No," he told them. Their tyee would be released after the release of the captives who were known to be at Friendly Cove.

After another uproar, Jewitt assumed the posture of Thompson and probably enjoyed it. "Kill me," he said, arching his chest outward. "I am only one among so many, and can make no resistance, but unless you wish to see your king hanging by his neck and sailors firing at him with bullets, you will not do it."

"Wik! Wik!" ("That must never be!"), they answered. For all their fury and threats, they wouldn't harm Jewitt and thereby risk losing their chief.

After the Nootka calmed down, Jewitt told them the plan. Thompson would board the ship and tell the captain to keep Maquina until the other captive was released. When Thompson objected, saying that he would not leave his son with the savages, Jewitt waved him off, saying that his father would go first. Maquina would be put in a boat, and the exchange of the chief and Jewitt would take place within shouting distance of the *Lydia*, so Jewitt could reach the ship before any trickery. The subchiefs wanted the exchange to take place on shore, to which Jewitt said, "Wik." Whatever else might be said about the captive, he was in command now.

Of course, he didn't explain all of his plan to the villagers. He let the subchiefs pick the paddlers, who were strong warriors, but they were to be unarmed while he had pistols hidden inside of his robe. The prince clung to Jewitt's arm on the way to the canoe, and Ya-tintla-no tried to assure him that no harm would come to his father. She didn't know that Jewitt was a good liar, and she trusted his judgment. She had no choice either.

So Jewitt boarded the canoe to freedom. During his captivity, he had written, "I felt it was my destiny never more to behold a Christian land," and he had also said his final prayers three times. Every Sunday, he had prayed for rescue, but he had never envisioned it happening so swiftly and with so little fanfare. Had his story been fiction, he might have wished for some drumming, a boom from the cannon, maybe a speech by Kinclemet. There was none of that because this was real life. The village was somber and quiet when Jewitt left, and so was he. He could be sentimental later.

As the canoe neared the *Lydia*, Jewitt drew his pistols and ordered the paddlers to continue. His intention was to board the ship and keep Maquina prisoner until the crew of the *Lydia* took the remaining loot from the *Boston* out of Maquina's village and loaded it onto the ship. When the canoe reached the *Lydia*, he secured his pistols, scrambled up the rope ladder, and rolled onto the deck. Captain Hill said that he had never seen such a strange creature, painted in black, wearing the fur of a bear, and with his hair dangling in a tuft. It was exactly how Jewitt viewed the Nootka two and a half years ago.

The bond between Jewitt and Maquina was evident when they met below deck. The chief was bound in irons and looked sad, but once he saw Jewitt, he brightened up, saying, "Wocash, John" ("Very good, John")!

When Jewitt had the irons removed, Maquina hugged him and repeated in a whisper, "Wocash. Wocash."

Jewitt wrote, "I felt sincere pleasure in freeing the chief from the irons, a man who had caused the death of my comrades, but who was my friend and protector." All true.

Jewitt's finest hour came in the next thirty minutes, while he was still below deck. Captain Hill asked that he give a complete account of the *Boston*. Once Jewitt finished, Hill called for Maquina's death, to even things out. A lesser person might have backed down, but Jewitt stood up to Hill. He recounted the offenses Maquina's people had suffered at the hands of whites and also said that the Nootka should be left alone, which was a miraculous statement for the time. Seeing that Hill was unmoved, he stole a scene from Ya-tintla-no, the one in which she had saved his life. "I have lived long enough with these people to know that revenge is held sacred," he said, "and they will not fail to retaliate should their king be killed." In tears, he declared, "I will not take the life of a man who has preserved mine." Hill was moved to let Maquina go.

The chief understood that his friend was trying to save his life, but he didn't think that he would be successful. Worse, he was in turmoil every time Thompson's name was mentioned. At each instance, Maquina asked if Thompson wished to kill him, to which Jewitt kept saying, "Wik, wik," over and over. There was no bond between Thompson and the chief, and Maquina was right to fear him, but not now, not in 1805. Thompson was tired and just wanted to drink rum.

The last entry in Jewitt's journal was predictably emotional and important as a final observation about the Nootka. After the loot from the *Boston* was on the *Lydia* and Maquina was released, the two men embraced for some time, as if not wanting to part. The chief whispered, "Tooteyoohannis, klushish" ("John, good").

Jewitt whispered back, "Klooskosh Tyee" ("Great Chief"), and said in the Nootka language that Maquina should care for his people and feed many visitors. "Then grasping both of my hands," Jewitt said, "with much emotion, while tears trickled down his cheeks, he bade me farewell." Of his escape and view of the Nootka in 1805, Jewitt wrote:

> Notwithstanding the joy at my deliverance, and the pleasing anticipation I felt of once more beholding a civilized country, and again being permitted to offer up my devotions in a Christian church, I could not avoid experiencing a painful sensation on parting with the savage chief. He had preserved my life and treated me with kindness, and considering Nootka ideas and manners, I could have fared much worse.

The *Lydia* proceeded north for trading. As it set sail from Friendly Cove, Jewitt could hear drumming on the houses and the chorus of "Wocash, Tyee! Wocash, Tyee!" The vision of Maquina's returning to his people touched Jewitt's heart, and the readers of his book were glad his story had a happy ending. He was headed for a "civilized county" and was no longer at the mercy of a "savage chief."

Afterword

I t is not clear how much Jewitt changed during his captivity. He had deep feelings for Maquina, but he still called him a "savage chief." He had grown to appreciate some parts of Nootka culture, but he was eager to return to a "civilized country." When his heart was speaking, he was moved by the basic humanity of the Nootka. When he compared their way of life to his, he saw them as less than human. He certainly knew who the Nootka were in 1803—"savages." By 1805, he was less certain and didn't know his own mind.

As for Thompson, he appeared to be worn out from living a life based on ignorance and rage. Had he lived with the Nootka for thirty years, he wouldn't have changed. Jewitt might have. It might have finally occurred to him that his people were once like the Nootka in their religious beliefs, in their method of waging war, and in the way they dressed. He may have gained the insight that introducing metal products into their culture wasn't very helpful to their development. But in the end, Jewitt learned the solution to the horrors of the China Trade: whites should leave people in other parts of the world alone.

Perhaps it is unfair to judge Jewitt's prejudice from today's perspective, but it can't be avoided. If each generation seeks to improve humanity and not repeat mistakes, then judgments must be made and lessons learned. The great mistake in Jewitt's age was that white people thought that their culture was superior to all other cultures and that their race was superior to all other races, and then they used these conclusions to justify enslaving Africans and killing Native Americans. To ignore this mistake and fail to learn from it would be equal to repeating the tragedies of the China Trade.

After trading along the coast for three months, the *Lydia* returned to Friendly Cove. Jewitt was greeted with the news that Yuqua had given birth to a son and that he was the father. He wasn't moved one way or the other and made no attempt to see his former wife or his son. Instead, he told Maquina that he wouldn't be back, whereupon the chief said that he would raise the boy as his own tyee. It was a victory for Yuqua. She had achieved her goal, as now she was guaranteed to be respected and protected by a powerful chief.

The *Lydia* reached China and exchanged its skins for silk, spices, and tea. At the port of Canton, Jewitt met a childhood friend who conveyed the news that everyone back home thought he was dead. When he learned that the friend was a crewman on a ship bound for Hull, Jewitt's home, he gave the man a letter to carry to his father, in which he spoke of his captivity and subsequent rescue. Upon the *Lydia*'s arrival in Boston, Massachusetts, in June 1807, Jewitt was given a stack of letters from his father and friends back home.

Not long after arriving in Boston, Jewitt published his journal under the title *A Journal Kept at Nootka Sound*. When he wasn't working as a blacksmith, he traveled to promote the book. In 1809, he married Hester Jones, a native of England, and afterward they moved to Connecticut, where his book caught the eye of Richard Alsop, an accomplished writer. With Alsop's help in editing the journal and expanding on Nootka culture, Jewitt published the account a second time in 1815, this one titled *A Narrative of the Adventures and Sufferings of John R. Jewitt while Held as a Captive of the Nootka*

Indians of Vancouver Island, 1803 to 1805. It was an instant success. Three editions were published in the first year, and nine thousand copies sold in the first two years, a remarkable record for the time.

A year later, the book piqued the interest of the playwright James Barker, who lived in Philadelphia. The result was a play called *The Armourer's Escape; or, Three Years at Nootka Sound,* which opened in Philadelphia in 1817 with Jewitt playing the lead roles. He dressed as Maquina and reenacted war, then he changed clothes to play himself. The play was successful. It also promoted the stereotype of the Natives as savages.

Jewitt never returned to England and, therefore, never saw his father again. His marriage produced three sons and two daughters, but he didn't live to see his children grow up. Often complaining of headaches from the wound to his head, John Rodgers Jewitt died on January 7, 1821, at the age of thirty-seven. His and Yuqua's son produced grandsons, who have carried the name John Rodgers Jewitt into the twenty-first century. Jewitt and Hester's sons have carried his name to the present day. Most of his and Hester's descendants live in Connecticut.

Thompson never made it home to Philadelphia. He caught malaria in Havana, Cuba, and died there. Little is known about Maquina after 1805. Because of the massacre of the *Boston,* ships continued to avoid Friendly Cove. The last reference to the chief was written in 1825, when a trader referred to Maquina as "an aging man." Nootkan oral tradition relates that the chief was killed during a raid on a nearby village.

In 1846, the United States fought a war with Mexico and acquired California. For the next thirty years, much of the trade with China was conducted through the port of San Francisco, which helped give rise to the city of San Francisco. By the 1880s, the seal and otter along the California coast had been depleted, and England was conducting trade with China, exchanging opium for silk and spices.

The gold rush in 1849 brought an influx of whites to Vancouver Island. The Nootka fought the intrusion, but smallpox reduced their population by more than half in just a few years. Vancouver Island became a British colony, and in 1866 it became part of the province of British Columbia. Canada seized the land, forcing the Natives to live on reservations. Currently, the Nootka population on the island is about six thousand, and many sustain themselves by working in canneries and in the logging industry.

The island is marked by several references to Jewitt and Maquina. The pond where Jewitt spent his Sundays is called Jewitt's Lake. Boston Point was named in memory of the ill-fated ship, and the modern town of Tahsis was named after Maquina's autumn village. Several streets have been named after people who were connected to the *Boston*—Jewitt, Maquina, and Tootoosch.

Jewitt's original journal was lost. There is some evidence that he may have sent it to his father in 1809. Since its publication in 1815, *A Narrative of the Adventures and Sufferings of John R. Jewitt* has been reprinted in twenty-two editions, including a German translation. It is still considered one of the best firsthand accounts of Native Americans before their cultures were modified after contact with whites.

Recently, the Nootka of Vancouver Island have discussed whether or not they might resume hunting whale to connect their culture with the past. "It would take a great revival of traditional skills," a spokesman said, as they would want to use the same canoes and weapons Maquina used. With a harpoon made of yew wood and coils of cedar rope, they would paddle into the ocean and sing to the whale, as their ancestors had for thousands of years:

> Whale, we have given you what you are wishing to get—a good harpoon. Please hold it with your strong hands and do not let go. Whale, turn toward the beach and you will see the people who have come to greet you. They will say, "What a great whale you are! What a fat whale you are!" And you, whale, will be proud of your greatness.

> We are glad you have come to visit us. We have been saving these feathers for you for a long time. Take them and wear them to show your greatness. *Great whale! Great whale!* Klooskosh mah-hack! Klooskosh mah-hack!

BIBLIOGRAPHIC NOTE

The University of Washington at Seattle and the University of British Columbia at Vancouver hold most of the twenty-two editions of John Jewitt's journal. Most commonly called *A Narrative of the Adventures and Sufferings of John R. Jewitt*, other titles include *Adventures and Sufferings of John R. Jewitt* and *Captive of Nootka; or, The Adventures of John R. Jewitt* and *White Slaves of the Nootka: Narrative of the Adventures of John R. Jewitt*.

Many editions of the journal contain valuable annotations and bibliographic information, although not all editors accept Jewitt's account as completely accurate. For example, some argue that there is evidence that he married a commoner, not Yuqua, who was a princess. Others disagree. *Among the Nootka* uses information from several editions to reconcile discrepancies and also relates Jewitt's account of his marriage to Yuqua as described in *A Narrative of the Adventures and Sufferings of John R. Jewitt* (Ramona, CA: Ballena Press, 1975), edited by Robert F. Heizer, which contains annotations and an extensive introduction.

For Jewitt's original journal published in 1807, see John Rodgers Jewitt, *Captive of the Nootka Indians: The Northwest Coast Adventures of John R. Jewitt*, edited by Alice Shurcliff and Sarah Shurcliff Ingelfinger (Boston: Back Bay Books, 1993; distributed by Northeastern University Press), pp. 112–130; and John Rodgers Jewitt, *A Journal Kept at Nootka Sound* (Fairfield, WA: Ye Galleon Press, 1988).

Frederick W. Howay brings the attack on the *Boston* into perspective in his work "Indian Attacks upon Maritime Traders of the Northwest Coast, 1785–1805" in *Canadian Historical Review* 6 (1925), pp. 287–309. For other accounts of the *Boston*, see Frederick W. Howay, "An Early Account of the Loss of the *Boston* in 1803," *Pacific Northwest Quarterly* 17 (1926), pp. 280–88, and David Savage, "Massacre at Nootka Sound," *British Columbia Digest* (April 1946), pp. 14–17.

Eleanor H. Broadus, in *John Jewitt, The Captive of Nootka* (Toronto: Ryerson Press, 1928), provides a fictionalized account of Jewitt's captivity. Shannon Garst's *John Jewitt's Adventure* (Boston: Houghton Mifflin, 1955) and Agnes C. Laut's *The Boy John Jewitt* (no place, no date; held in Special Collections at the University of British Columbia) are popular and unscholarly. See also E. S. Meany Jr., "The Later Life of John R. Jewitt," *British Columbia Historical Quarterly* 4 (July 1940), pp. 143–63. For other accounts of white people who were held in captivity by Native Americans, see the excellent bibliography in Marius Barbeau's "Indian Captivities," *Proceedings of the American Philosophical Society* 94, no. 6 (December 1950), pp. 522–48.

Philip Drucker is the leading authority on Nootkan culture. Among his most useful works are *Cultures of the North Pacific Coast* (San Francisco: Chandler Publishing Company, 1965); *Indians of the Northwest Coast* (Garden City, NY: Natural History Press, 1963); and "The Northern and Central Nootkan Tribes" in *Indians of the Pacific Coast*, edited by Tom McFeat (Seattle: University of Washington Press, 1966), pp. 22–27. Other sources include Ruth Kirk, *Wisdom of the Elders: Native Traditions on the Northwest Coast* (Vancouver:

Douglas and McIntgre Ltd., 1986); Gilbert M. Sproat, *Scenes and Studies of Savage Life* (London: Smith Elder, 1868); and Earl H. Swanson, "Nootka and the California Gray Whale," *Pacific Northwest Quarterly* 47 (January 1956), pp. 52–56. For further information on Native Americans and whaling, see Robert F. Heizer's "A Bibliography of Aboriginal Whaling," *Society for the Bibliography of Natural History* 4 (1968), pp. 344–362.

Where spelling discrepancies occurred between Jewitt's journal and the annotations of his account, the author chose the word easiest to pronounce—most notably, "Maquina" over "Maquinnah"; "Ya-tintla-no" over "Y-Ya-tintla-no"; "Kinclemet" over "Kinneclimmets"; and "Utilla" over "Ulatilla." In this book, the author has elaborated on aspects of Nootkan culture that are mentioned in Jewitt's account and has also edited some quotations for clarity.

Printed in the United States
By Bookmasters